Leisure Arts 14

Painting Boats & Harbours in Oils

Clifford Bayly

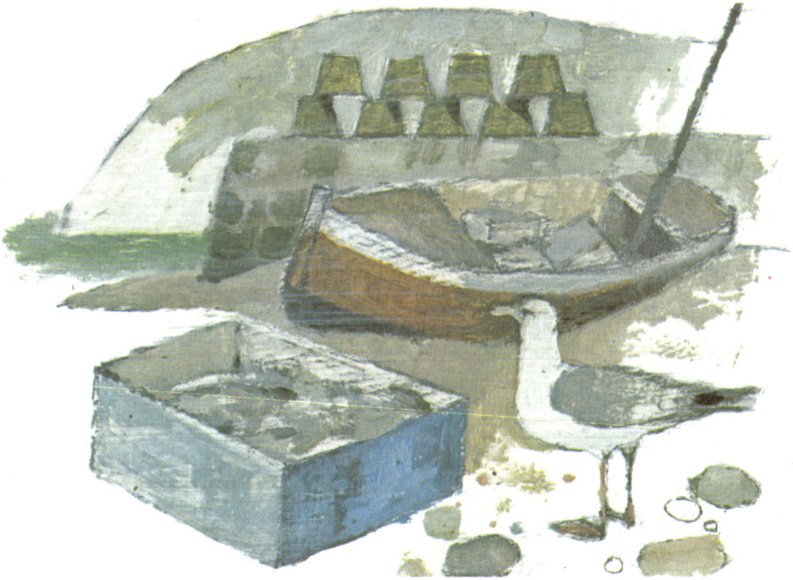

SEARCH PRESS LIMITED
London and Tunbridge Wells

TAPLINGER PUBLISHING CO., NEW YORK
A Pentalic Book

METHUEN AUSTRALIA

Introduction

Boats and harbours are two of my favourite subjects. I have lived and worked near the sea for many years and have absorbed an abiding interest in and fascination with the visual qualities that exist in the panoramas and even in the bric-à-brac which are always associated with it.

Of all the natural elements the sea is the most powerful in leaving its mark on everything with which it comes into contact. It influences the appearance of other natural materials such as sand, stone and wood by shaping, colouring, eroding and bleaching. Its effects upon man-made materials such as metal, paint and rope add texture and character even by virtue of its corrosive and abrasive action. In studying and painting boats and harbours an appreciation of the visual qualities of these various materials is essential. I would encourage the reader to draw and paint on the spot as much as possible. I know it can be very inconvenient – particularly with incoming tides and blowing sand to say nothing of the occasional pungent smell of fish! Keep your painting gear to a minimum but take the precaution of using a small folding seat or stool and if possible a light sketching easel as it is difficult to work satisfactorily whilst sitting on wet sand or cold rocks.

Although we are concerned principally with the painting of boats and harbours it is essential that the context in which they exist is authentic and supports the character of the subject. I should add, in this connection, that in this book I am relating boats and harbours to the sea rather than to rivers or lakes, but either way the same principles apply.

On the subject of painting boards, I always prepare my boards with a ground according to the texture I wish to cover. This is usually brushed on in an acrylic primer.

Boats

There is no better way of gaining a basic knowledge of boats' form and function than by drawing them at first hand. Look carefully at their construction: for example, the line of the keel, whether flat or curved (that is if the boat is out of the water), the line of the gunwale or top edge of the sides. Check the proportion of beam (width) with the length, the angle of the bows (sharp end) etc. It is useful to draw a side view, back view and, if possible, a plan view first to establish the overall form before attempting the three-quarters view.

Although knowledge of boats and their rigging helps to give authenticity to your work remember that too much attention to detail can make a painting appear sterile. Try to capture atmosphere and mood and let detail remain subservient to the whole picture.

Harbours

It is not possible to cover the wide variety of harbours that exist – marinas, ports and docks. You will find that I have kept, in the main, to the smaller fishing harbours.

The materials with which most harbours are built present many different textural qualities which are worth some practice to represent effectively: stone slabs, rough stone, timber supports, cast concrete to name but a few. The variety of construction, particularly the methods of laying stones, is worth study. It varies with the locality of course – depending upon the material available and local methods of building. Subsidiary elements such as harbour lights and furniture sheds, small buildings, nets, fish-boxes and other marine gear lying about, also offer resonant subjects.

The sea

Consider the physical characteristics of sea, sky and land in their most basic form and look at their visual relationship to each other.

The sky influences both the sea and the land; shadows will be cast by any clouds that come between the sun and the surface of either sea or land. Land forms may be reflected in the sea in parts, and the sea in some areas will reflect the sky. This interaction means in practical terms that some sky colours will be found in the sea as will some land colours. The sky on the underside of clouds, on the other hand, will reflect something of the coolness of the sea colour where they are above it but over the land they will reflect the warmer land colours.

Notice how wind, and the resulting wave patterns formed, affect the tone and line of the sea, as does the seabed in shallower water. Boat hulls and sails reflected in the water's surface often show up almost to the same line: likewise bright light bouncing off the sea's surface affects the colour of harbour walls and ships.

Harbour scene: demonstration

Size: 265 × 265 mm/10½ × 10½ in. Brushes: Nos. 2 and 5 hog-hair; Nos. 2 and rigger sable. Colours: cobalt blue, ultramarine, viridian, sap green, raw umber, Naples yellow, yellow ochre, cadmium red.

In this demonstration (pages 4–5) I am attempting to illustrate the points already described by bringing together many of the components that feature in and around harbours into a hypothetical subject.

Stage 1 *(page 4)*

Using a rich coloured ground to give warmth to a predominantly blue-green subject, I draw over it the main compositional forms.

Stage 2

Blocking in the main areas I keep the tones as close as possible to those of the finished painting I have in mind. I make the general colour of the sea echo that of the sky, allowing the red ground to glint through. This prevents the overall effect from becoming too cool.

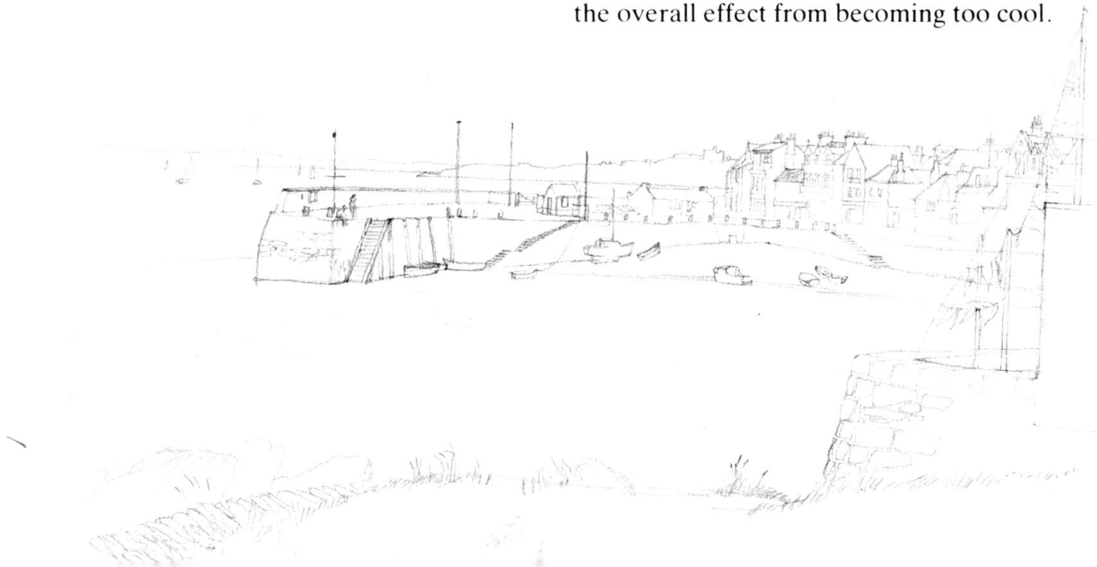

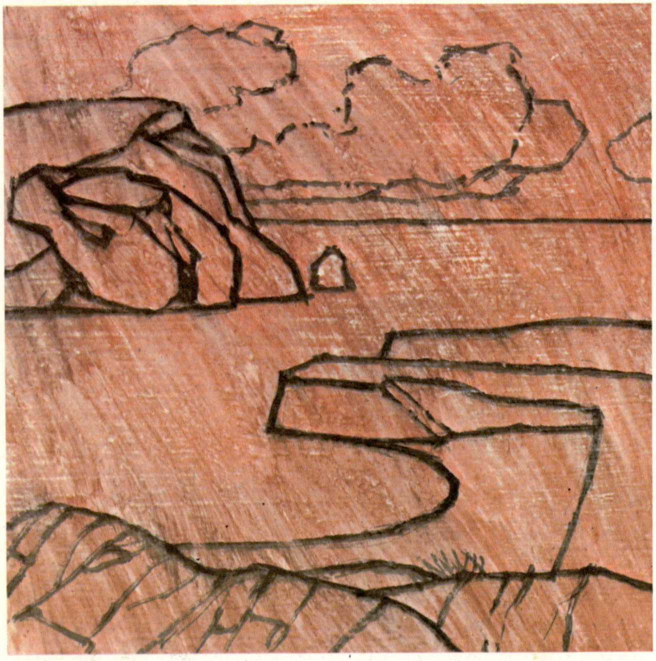

Stage 1

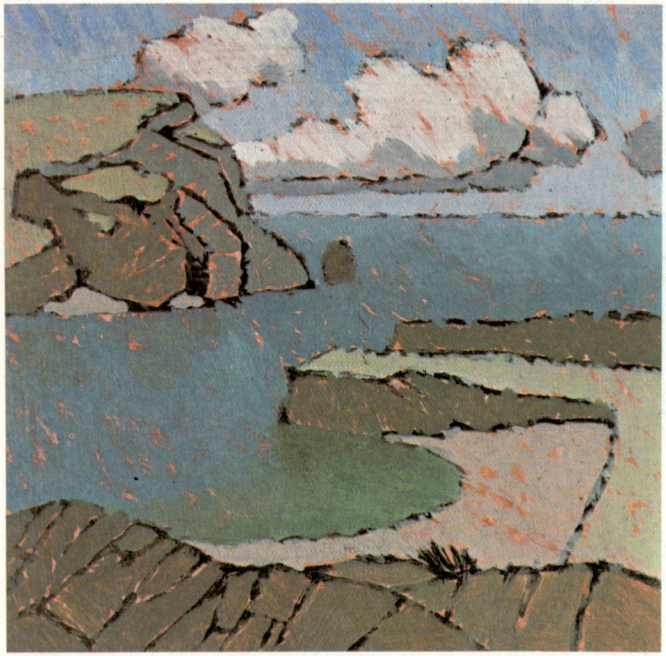

Stage 2

Stage 3

At this point I consider the influence of the sky on the sea, and indicate the shadow of the clouds on the sea's surface, the indirect reflections on it of the light clouds and cliffs, and the direct reflection of the harbour wall in the still water below it. Small plants in the foreground are then added to bring relief into the crags. I also put in the tide line on the harbour wall and the rocks where the seaweed clings to indicate that it is low tide.

Stage 4 – the finished painting

I now add the texture of the wind-ruffled water and the indirect cloud reflections more completely, and soften the cloud shadow. Notice how the sand under the very shallow water catches the sun, throwing up a clear, transparent blue green. Underwater rocks in this sandy bay are painted in with purple. I then modify the whole picture with touches of strong colour to help unify it and give the impression of an overall light source falling on all elements within the picture.

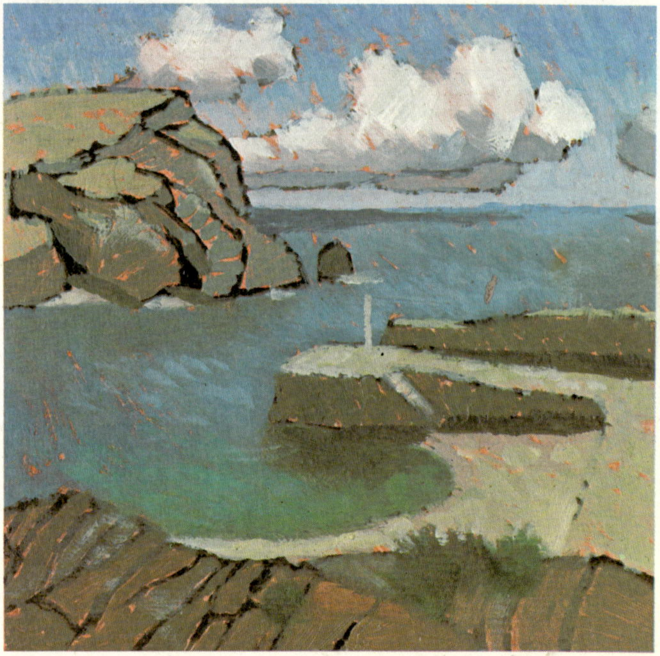

Stage 3

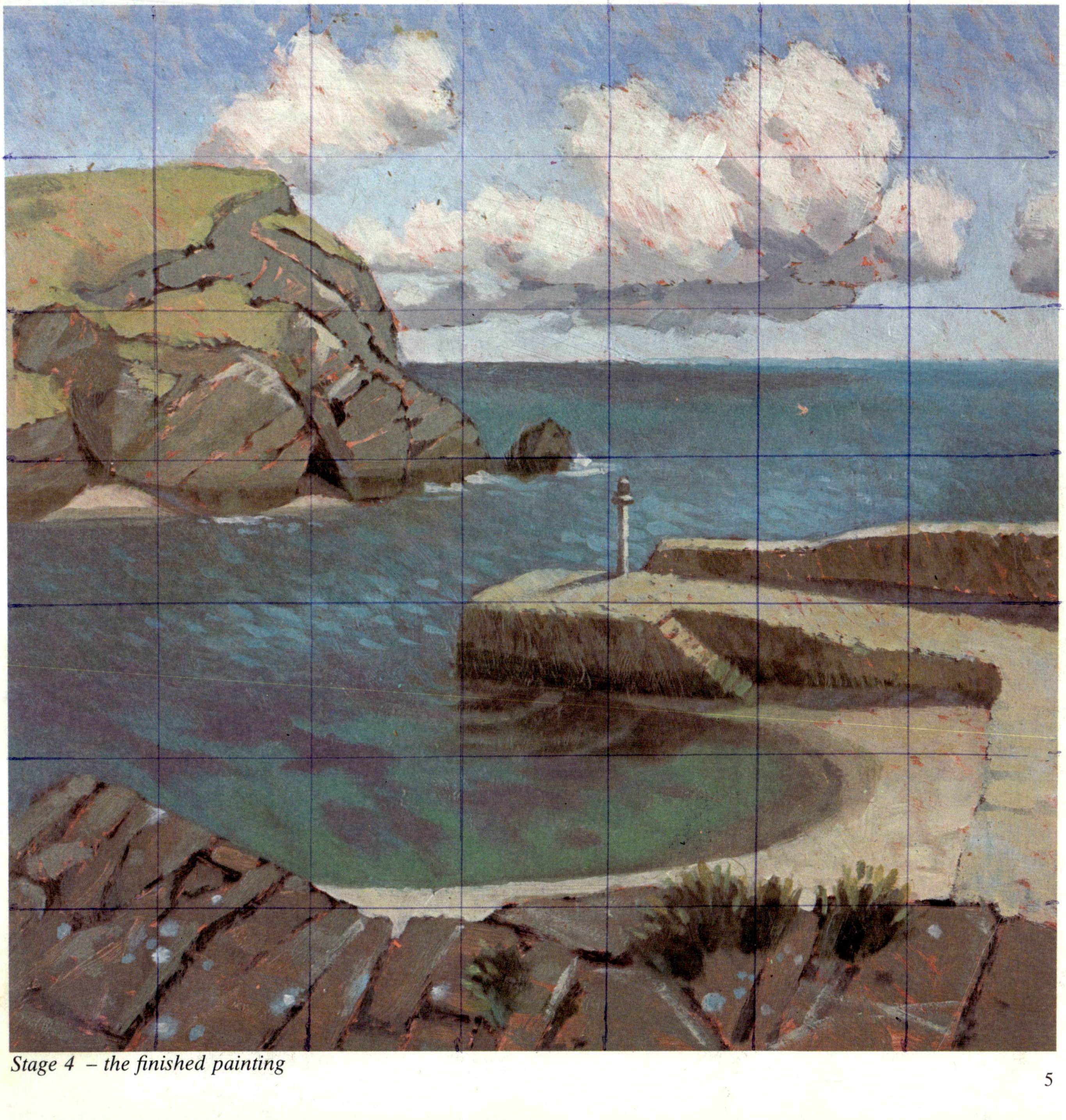

Stage 4 – the finished painting

Boats at Sea

The vastness of the sea is difficult to portray in paint. It is better, when first tackling subjects like this, to take just a portion of sea, and really study it thoroughly, making initial drawings and planning the angle and the scale of your boat subject.

The position from which you paint in relation to the sea and horizon is most important. If you are on a cliff-top (high angle) the horizon will appear level with your eyes, in which case there will be a large expanse of sea or beach in the foreground with very little sky area; and of course you look down onto most of the boats.

If you are standing or sitting on the beach (low angle), then again the horizon will be level with your eye height but the sea will become more of a strip along the bottom of the painting and boats will present a side view with masts and superstructure silhouetted against a larger area of sky. The lower angle gives a more intimate and dramatic aspect to your painting whilst the high angle suggests a more remote and serene atmosphere. These generalisations are, however, only a rough guide to setting up your picture; but remember that a horizon across the middle of a painting tends to make your subject static and dull.

Try to emphasise the character of your chosen boat type by placing it in the appropriate setting and if possible under typical weather conditions. This is not always easy to accomplish as the painting cannot be produced on the spot and one has to use drawings, colour notes and possibly photographs to complete it.

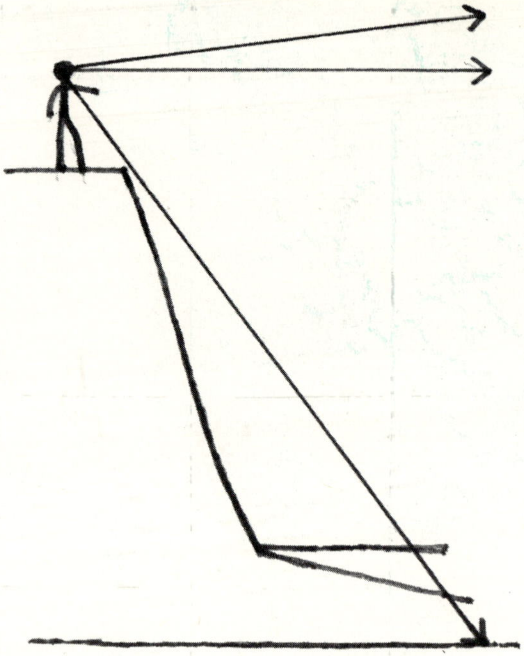

In the picture on pages 8–9 I tried to capture the nature of the hazards which fishing vessels undergo. To dramatise the subject I view it from the trough of a large wave that is pitching the boat headlong down it – into the picture, in fact. Such pictures can never be painted *in situ*; small sketchbooks and perhaps a camera will help to capture the essentials, but these can only be realised in the studio. Just a few compositional lines on an envelope gave me the inspiration for this painting.

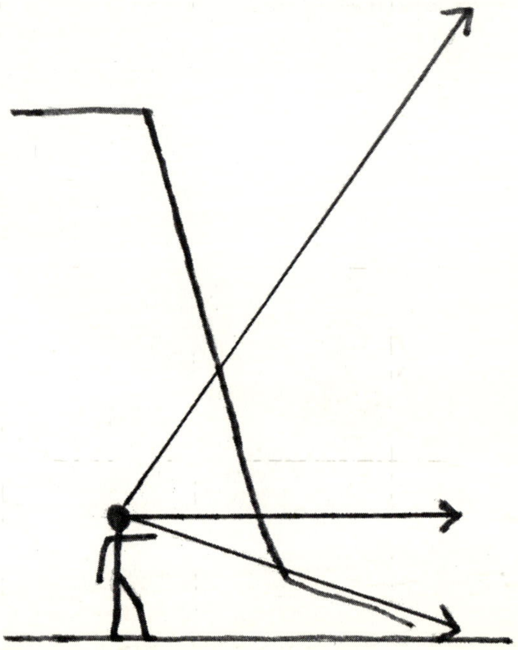

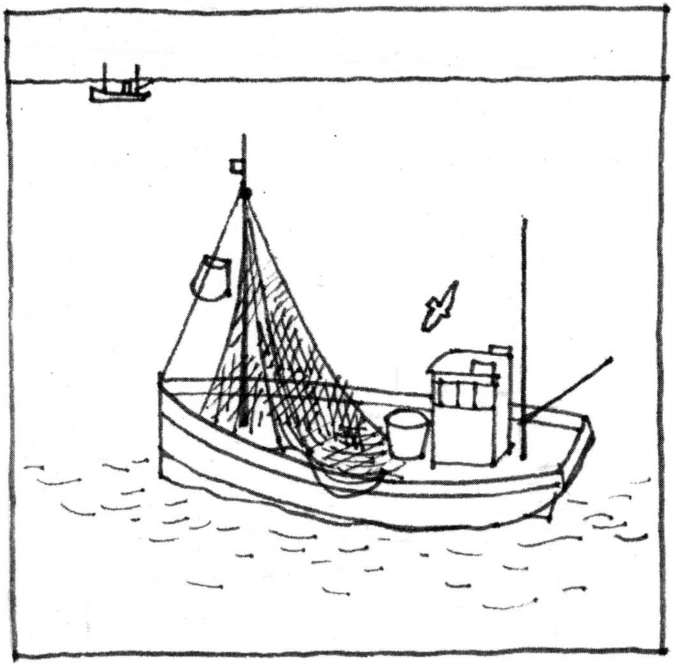

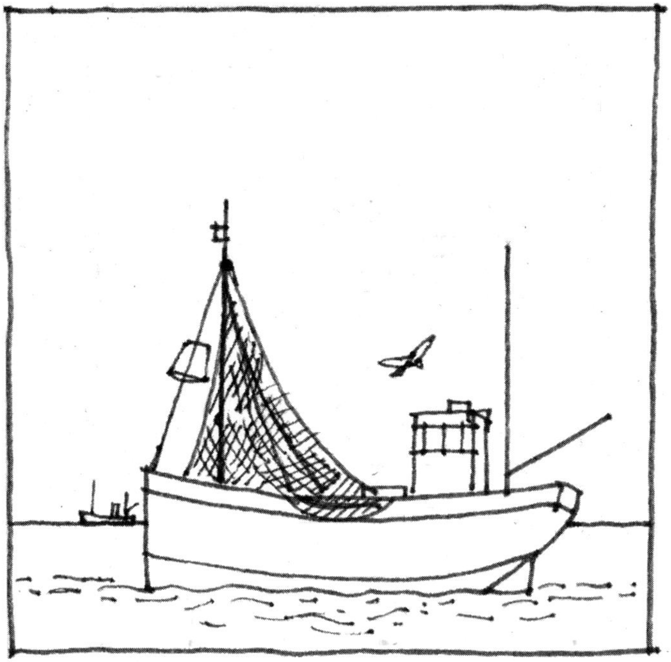

Rogue Wave: demonstration

Size: 265 × 265 mm/10½ × 10½ in. Brushes: Nos. 2 and 5 hog-hair; Nos. 2 and rigger sable. Colours: cobalt blue, viridian, permanent blue, sap green, cadmium red, yellow ochre.

Stage 1 *(page 8)*

I draw in the essential lines of the composition, making sure that the scale of the boat is correct in relation to the picture surface. These few lines dictate the drama and tension of the composition; once I have got them correct I can proceed with confidence.

Stage 2

As the lighting of the subject is the other essential ingredient in the composition, I work over it to enhance the dramatic effect started in Stage 1 with washes of thin permanent blue mixed with a little black.

Stage 3

I then add the basic subject colours to produce form and substance, light and atmosphere. For painting in the wave I use a dryish brush, dragging it over the underpainting and the ground to give a rough, broken texture.

Stage 4

To offset the overall coldness of the picture, I adjust the balance by painting in the brown of the hull and the dull reds of the rudder and the fishermen on deck. Foam trapped beneath the surface shows as a lighter green: I paint this by putting in the actual lines of foam and, when it is virtually dry, painting into them the elliptical areas which are formed as the foam disperses. (You can see this happening from the stern of harbour and cross-channel ferries.)

Stage 5 – the finished painting

I finally add the details of the boat, the small ships on the horizon, the seagulls and the flying foam, which I apply quite drily and loosely. Notice how the undersection of the hull picks up the colour of the foaming sea.

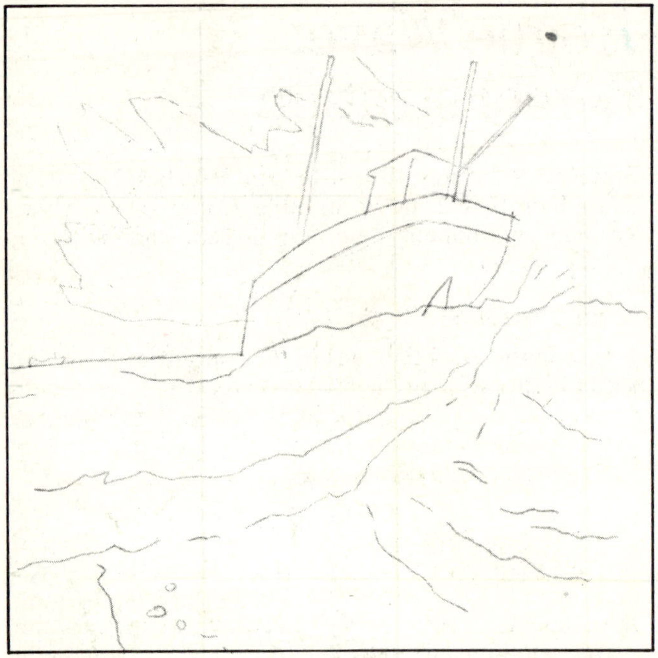

Stage 1

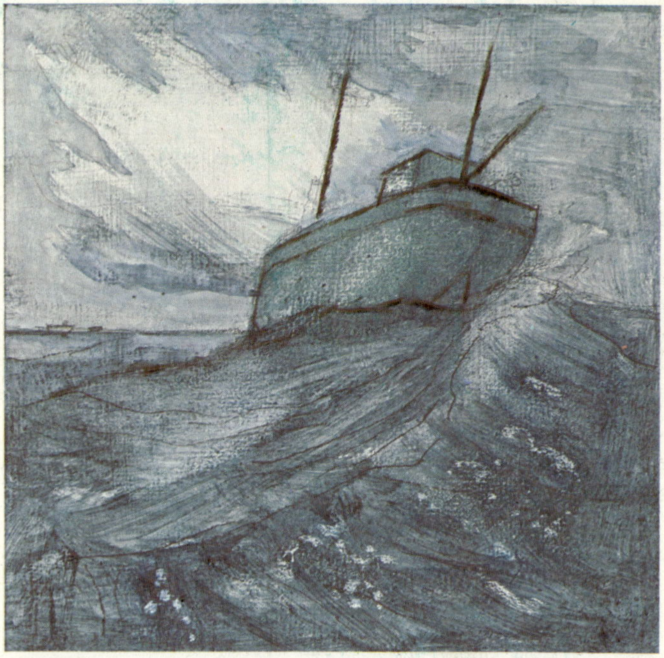

Stage 2

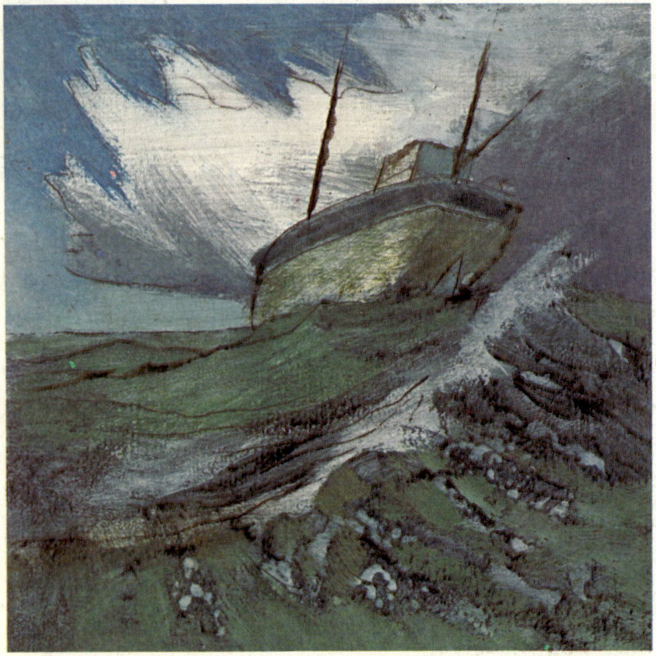

Stage 3

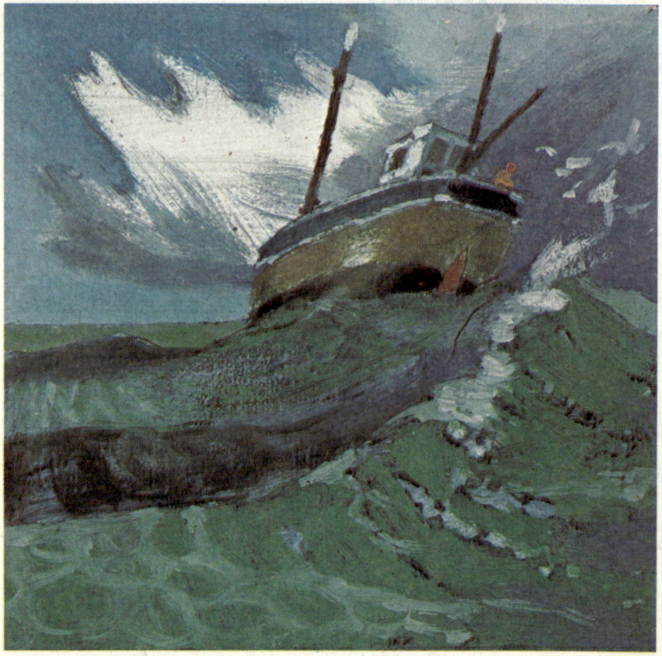

Stage 4

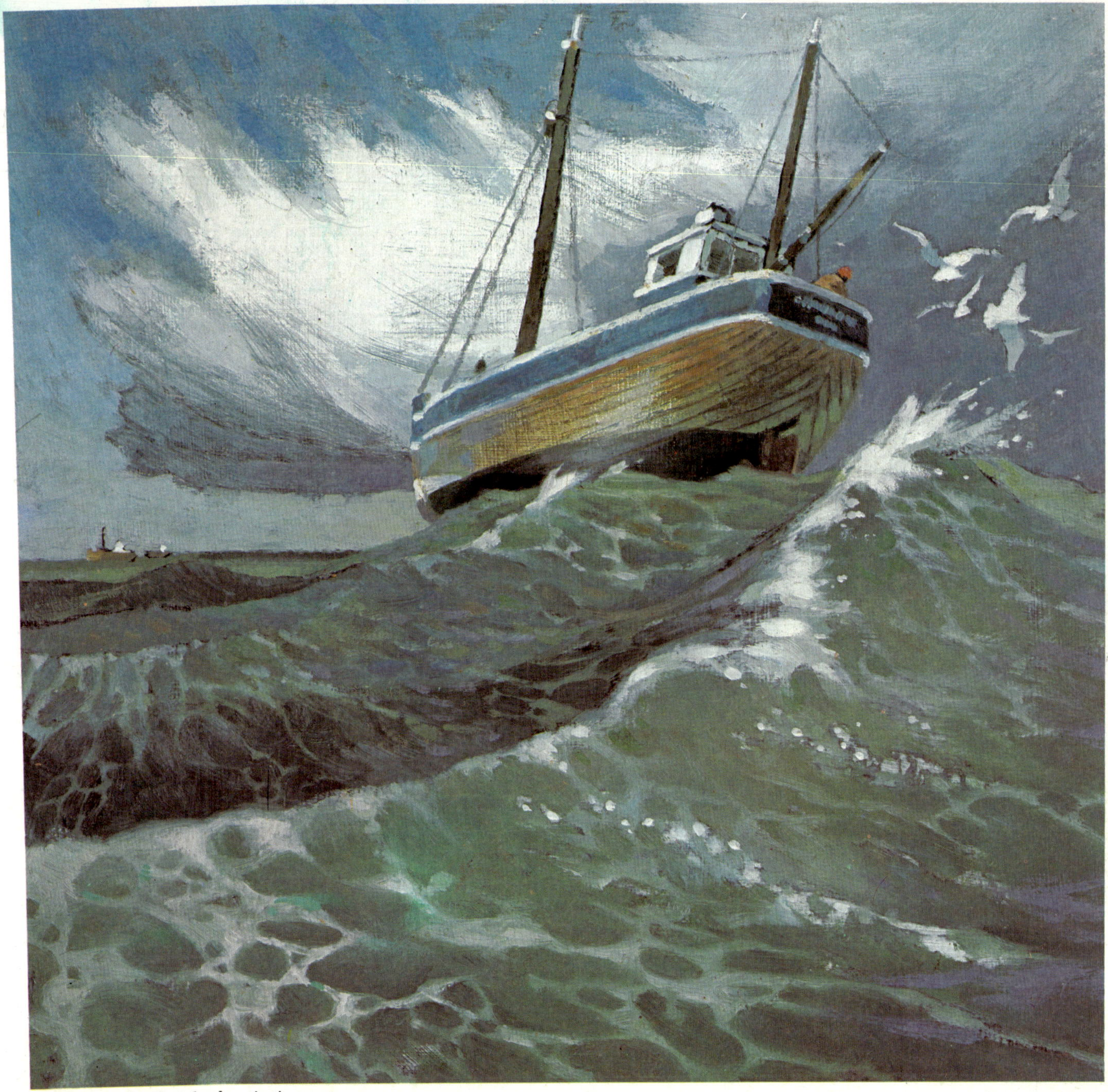
Stage 5 – the finished painting

Returning with the Catch

In this painting (pages 12–13) I chose to present a completely different viewpoint to the previous one. Both depict fishing boats – almost identical in fact – but I felt it would be helpful to show two contrasting aspects by using a completely different angle, context and colour.

The previous painting was a seascape with the elements dominating, the boat tossing about on a heavy sea. In this painting all is serene. It is evening. The water is calm. The fishermen's job is nearly finished for the day and their craft is slipping into harbour laden with the day's catch.

The diagonal lines in the first work suggested action and movement, whereas in this painting the verticals and horizontals contrast with each other to give a stabilised static quality. The lines of the jetty in the foreground serve to lead one into the picture and are gentle in character.

In this picture there is no horizon and no sky, but the evening sun is evident on the harbour walls, in the boats, and in the long shadows thrown by them.

Evening light, because it is so ephemeral, is best recorded by making written colour notes on sketches and by your memorising as far as possible the qualities of light and the forms that shadows take on when under very low light angles. Photographs too can help.

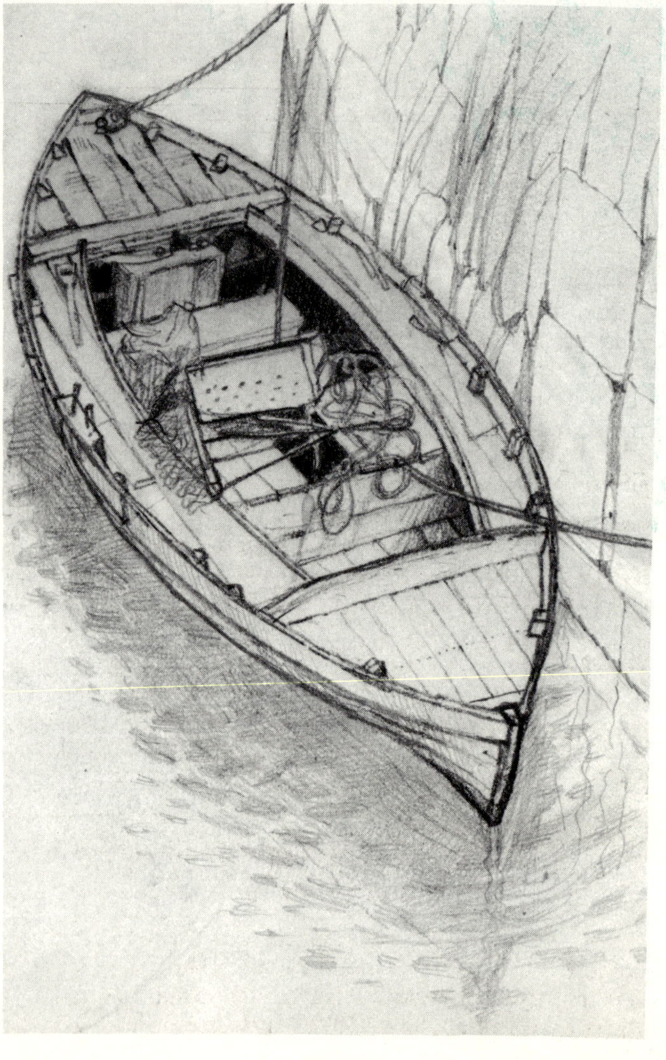

Returning with the Catch: demonstration

Size: 265 × 265 mm/10½ × 10½ in. Brushes: Nos. 2 and 6 flat hog-hair; No. 4 flat sable, rigger. Colours: permanent blue, sap green, Naples yellow, cadmium yellow, cadmium red, raw sienna, raw umber, cobalt blue.

Stage 1 ***(page 12)***

I quickly draw in the main subject forms in dark blue to capture the boat entering the harbour.

Stage 2

I now block in the general colours to create a warm evening glow, bearing in mind that certain areas will be picked out later in light warm colour where they catch the low evening sunlight. This means that most of the colour has to be rather rich and on the dark side.

Stage 3

I refine the colours and tones, paying particular attention to reflections and texture; and then deepen the water in the shadow areas and add richer tones generally to give contrast to the highlights.

Stage 4

At this point texture and detail become very much more important but they must be seen in relation to the whole atmosphere and mood of the painting. Small patches of colour – such as distant figures, the small boats, and detail on the larger boat – must not jump out of context and I keep the overall colour largely warm in character.

Stage 5 – the finished painting

I then work over the picture to establish the various textures. The wall behind the boat, although strongly textured, has to remain generally quite dark. The foreground wall needs to give the impression of the waning

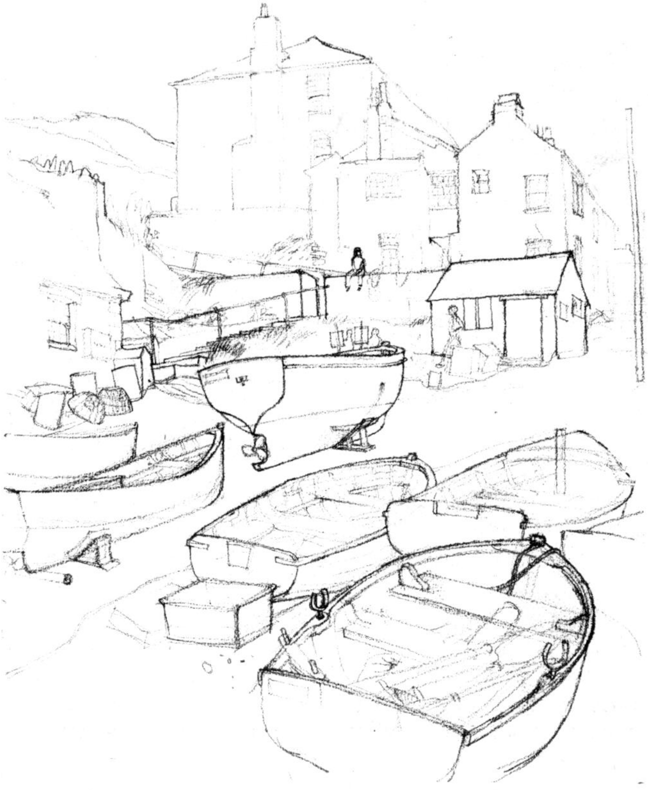

sun falling on one side while at the same time shining obliquely across the flat surface which in turn reflects something of the unseen sky colour. The deep and dark quality of the water is built up with successive layers of transparent colour, mainly sap green mixed with a little raw umber and, in the later layers, with a little cobalt blue as well.

I keep as much colour in the shadows as possible, otherwise they become sooty and dead and lose their luminosity. Never mix black with your base colour to produce a shadow colour. I keep shadow areas clean and luminous by increasing the intensity of the base colour with a small amount of its complementary or opposite colour – red to green, blue to orange, yellow to purple. Experiment with colour, using as little white and black as possible.

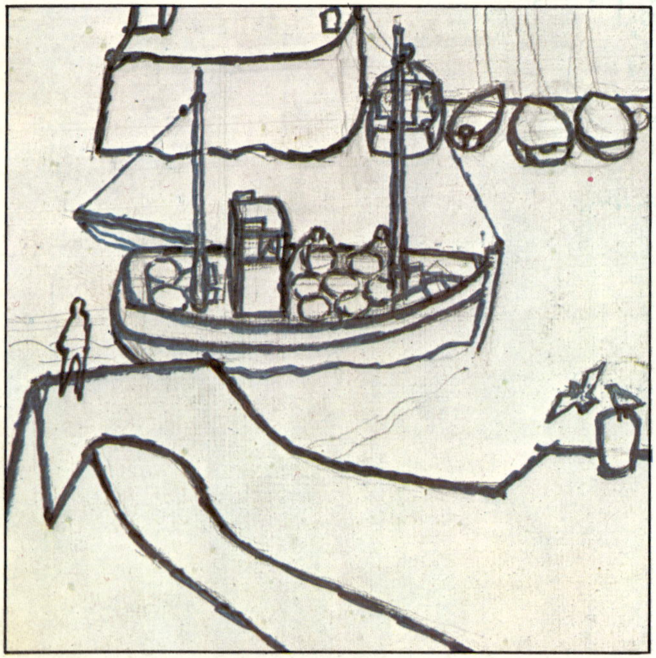

Stage 1

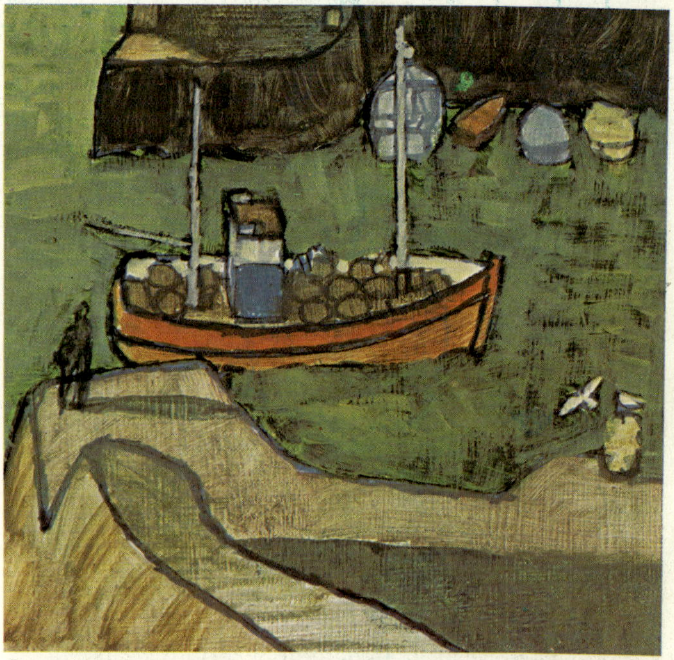

Stage 2

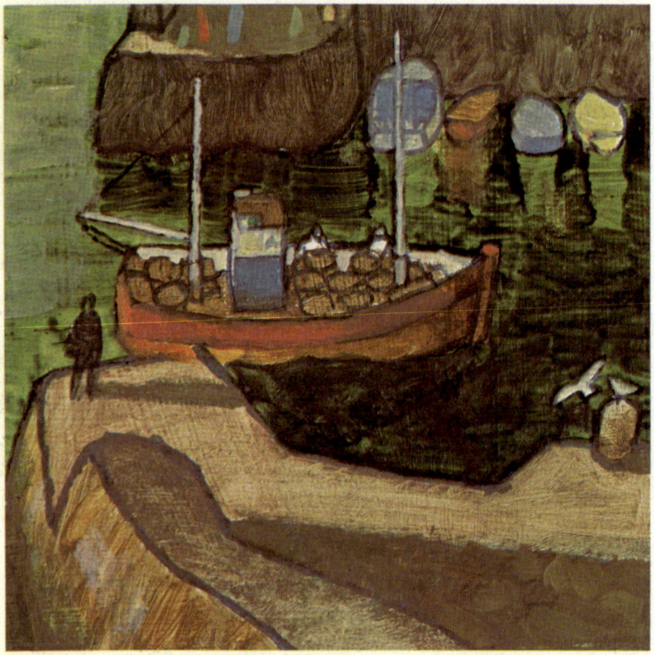

Stage 3

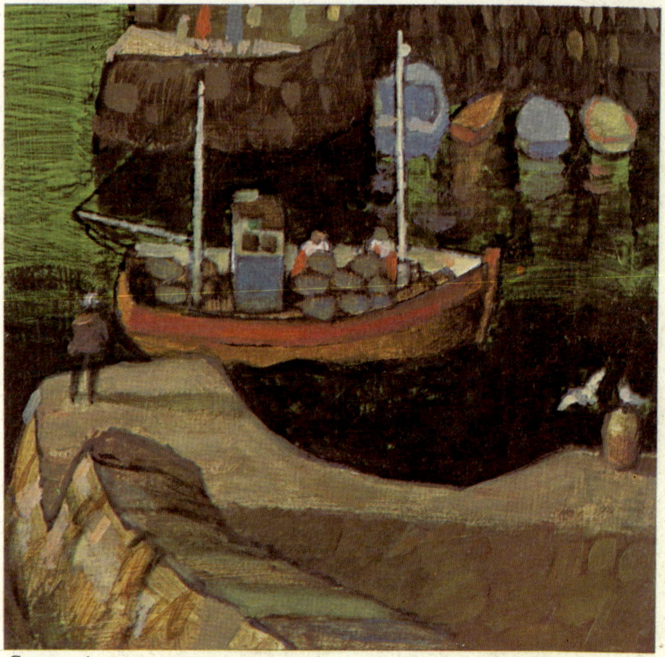

Stage 4

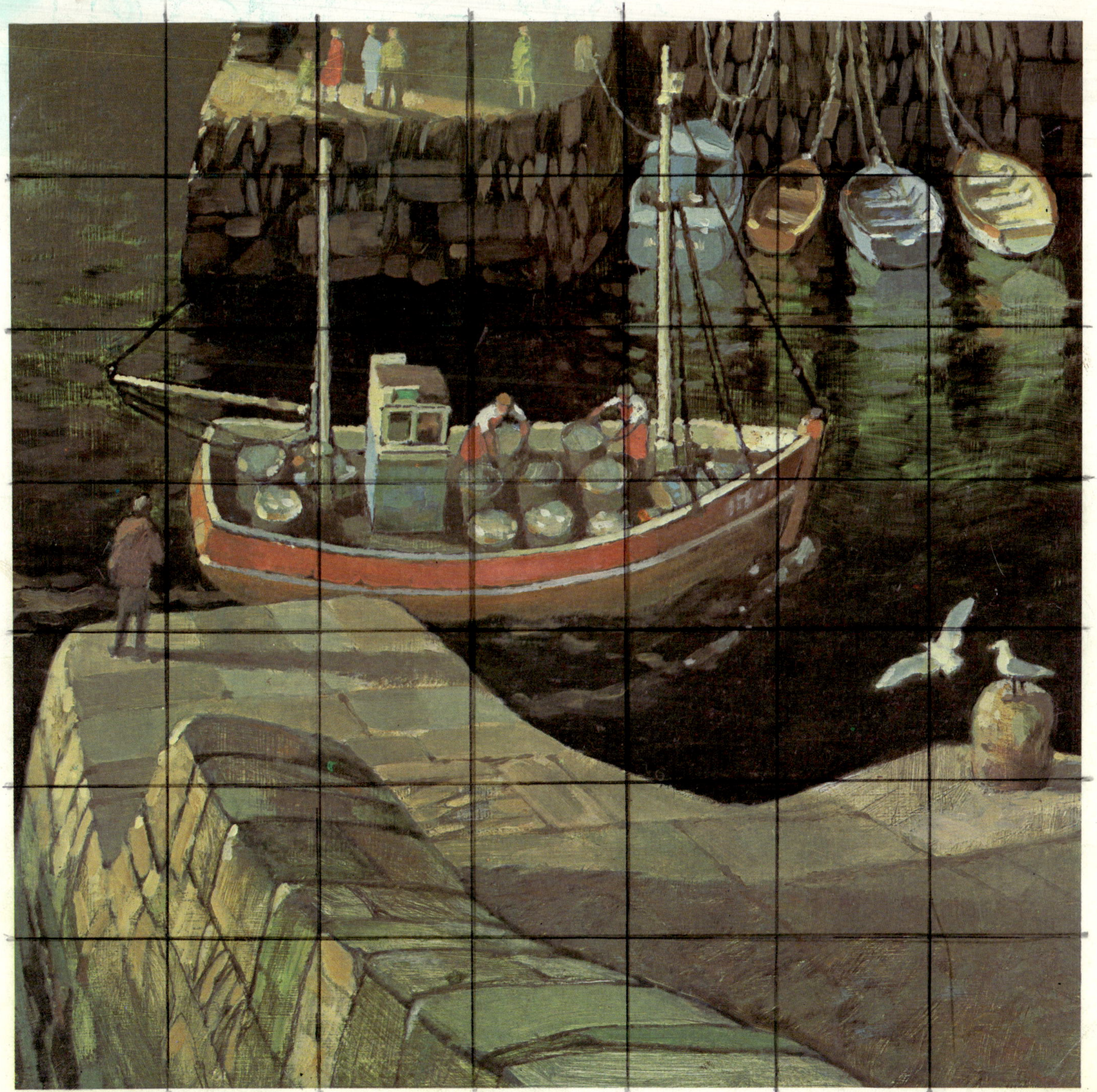

Stage 5 – the finished painting

The Harbour at low tide

Nothing is more serene, to my mind, than the sight of a small fishing harbour at low tide, with the boats lying on their sides or propped against the harbour wall as if asleep. Pools of water left by the receding tide give dramatic yet subtle contrasts against wet sand or mud, gulls perch on stones and wade across the mud looking for food. Human activity is generally confined to repairs, painting boats, and preparations for the incoming tide.

In previous demonstrations I have shown how bright sunlight, evening light, tide and sea have their effect on solids. In the next demonstration (pages 16–17) I attempt to show the underwater forms of stranded boats, and the effect of the bed of the harbour when left to dry out after the tide has receded.

Unless the wind is very strong, the shallow pools left by the tide have almost a mirror's surface, and so will reflect light from the sky or almost the very colour of objects that are near, though usually slightly darker. Wet mud and sand also pick up reflections, especially when viewed from ground level–a stretch of sand against strong sunlight can be almost dazzling, mud on a blue sunny day can pick up the azure of the sky, or retain some of the hull colour of a boat lying in it. When painting harbours at low tide look first for the tonal variations: this will help you to establish whether you have chosen the right viewpoint. Study the reflections, which will often break up what might appear first to be a series of dull, horizontal lines. In the studio, it is worthwhile practising reflections by using a model boat laid flat upon a mirror: that way one learns about basic principles and also about shadow formations as well. Remember not to confuse a reflection with a cast shadow.

Boats present different and exciting shapes when out of water and, seen from a low viewpoint when stranded or hauled out of the water for overhaul or storage, their shapes repay careful study, being essentially sculptural.

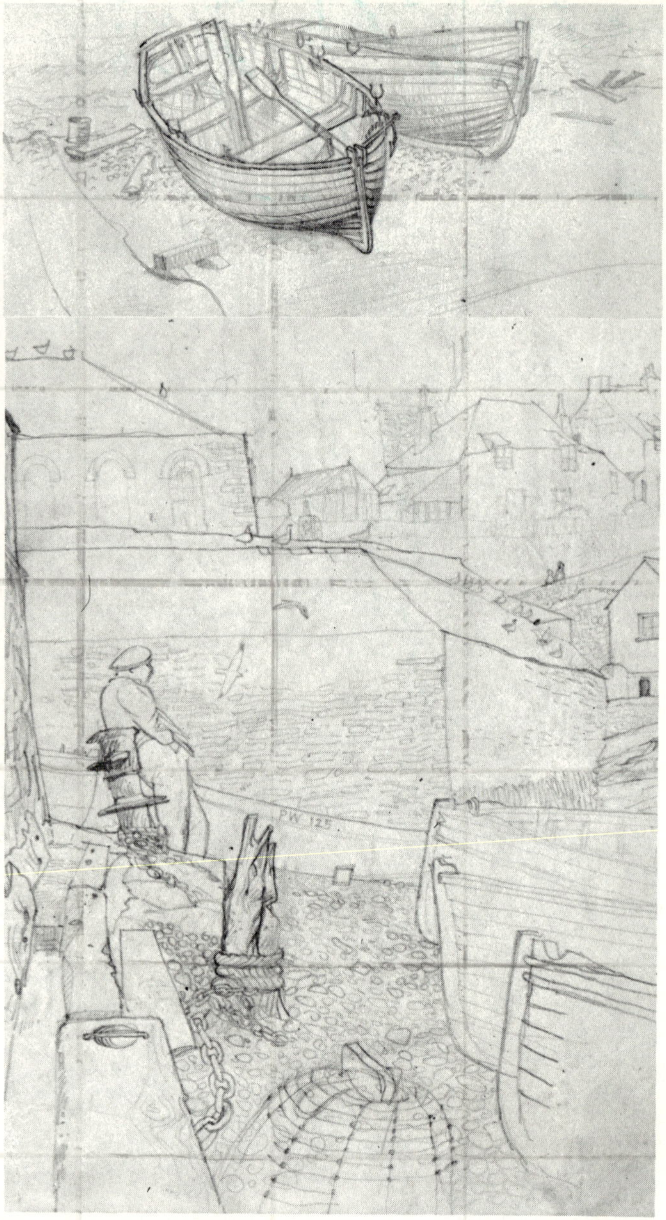

Notice how the hulls vary according to their function: wide and shallow for inshore work or, as with sailing boats, with deep keels to stabilise them.

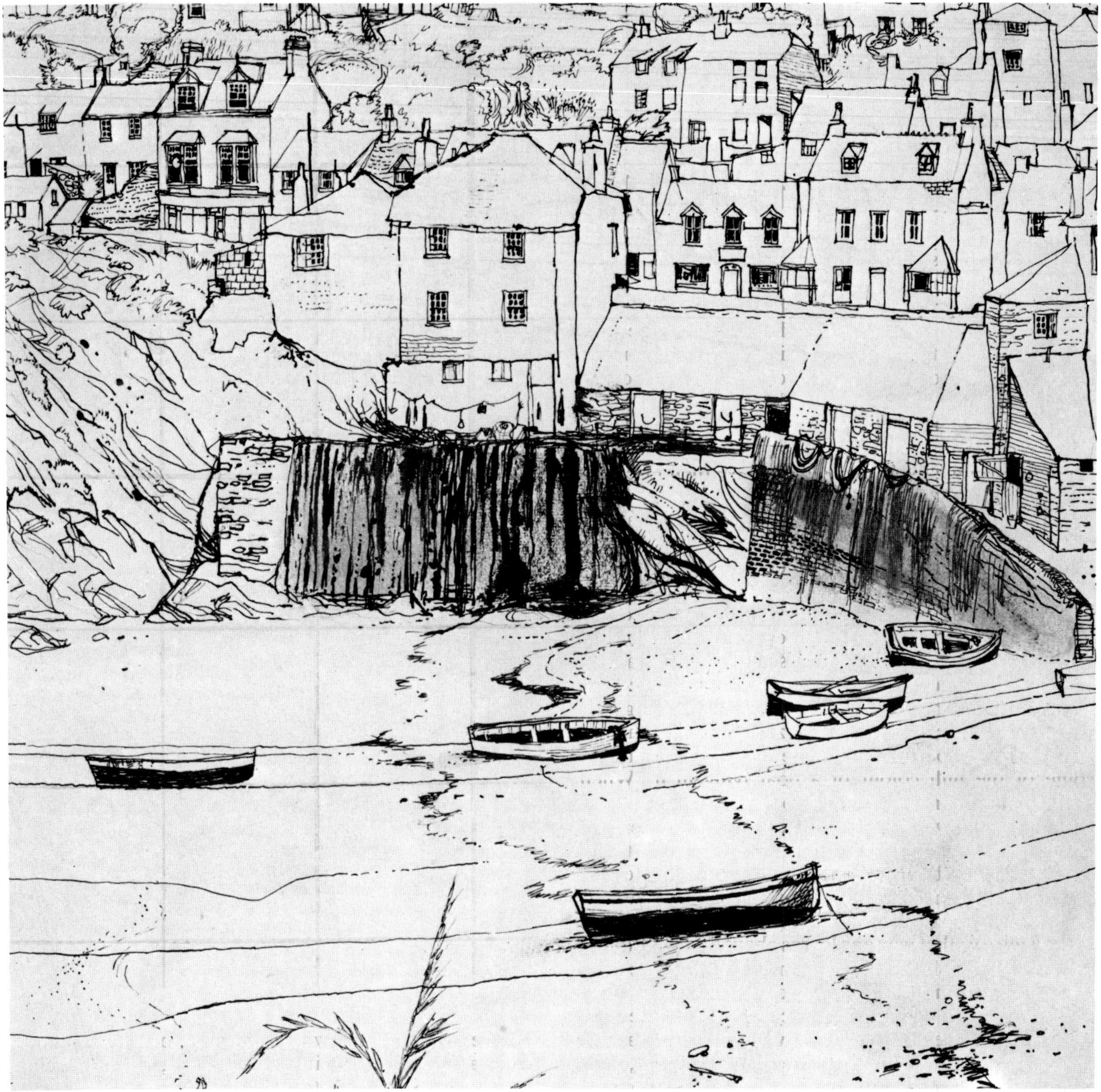

The Harbour at low tide: demonstration painting

Size: 431 × 266 mm/15 × 10½ in. Brushes: Nos. 2, 5, 8 flat sable; No. 2 round sable. Colours: Raw sienna, raw umber, Indian red, cobalt blue, yellow ochre, sap green.

An approaching storm makes the sky darker than the sea, which picks up the light from overhead. Likewise, the pools at the harbour entrance reflect indirect light cloud colour. I paint the wet mud in a light tone, picking out the little pools between my viewpoint and the boat on the right in light touches of colour, making sure to capture the dark reflection from the boat – a tone darker than that of the hull itself. When painting the blue and white boat, I make sure to get the correct tonal values of the side that is lying down: notice how reflected light from the mud gives it a warm tone. In the foreground, I paint in rocks and small stones, and also a line of seaweed left by the tide which gives contrast to the mud. Notice how I observe the shadow of the leg holding up the keelboat (top left): this emphasises the hull shape, giving it mass and form. Finally I paint in the gulls and the figures on the far quay, taking special care to make their respective sizes right, since they establish the size of the objects they are standing on, and create the correct sense of distance.

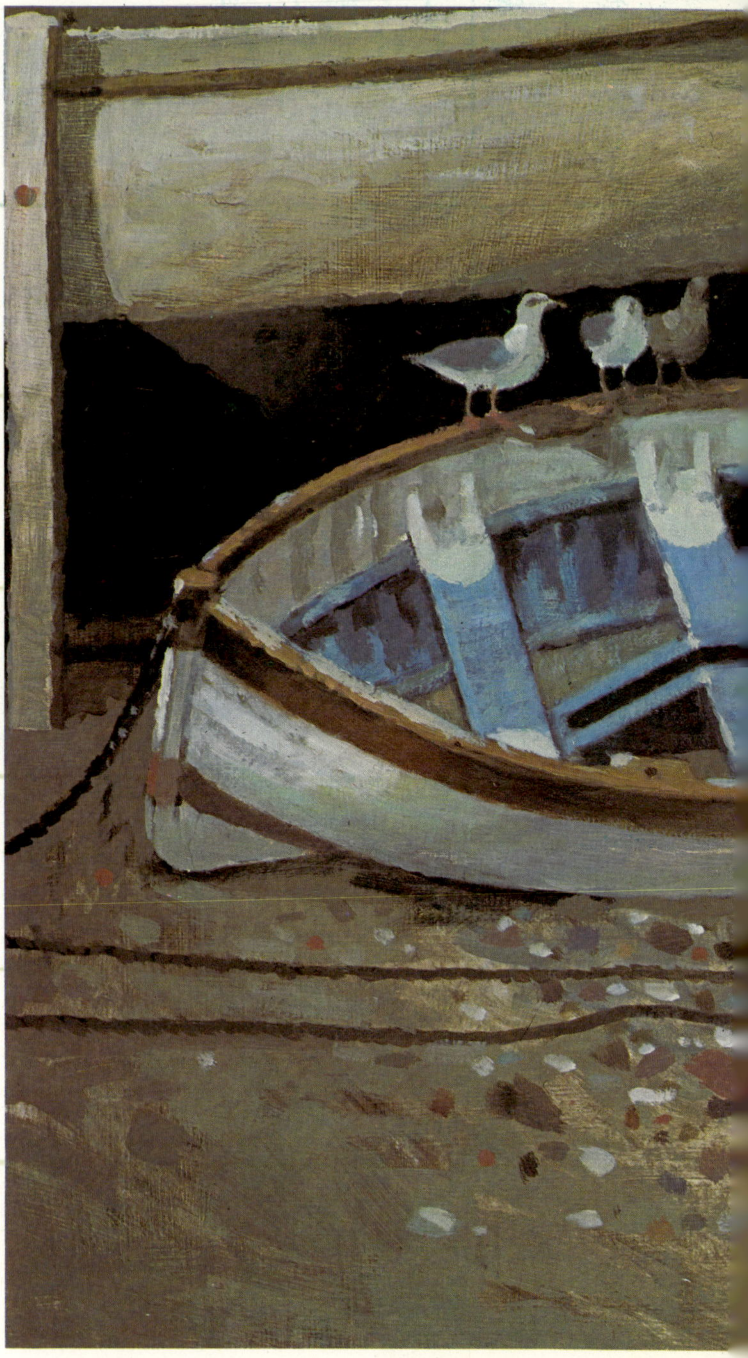

Port Isaac (see page 15)

I made this pen and ink sketch from a high viewpoint looking across the harbour at low tide as a possible drawing from which to paint the scene. Although the main interest is in the houses stacked up the steep hillside above the harbour wall, the lower half of the picture has enough contrast and interest to hold the picture together with its small boats and streaks left in the mud.

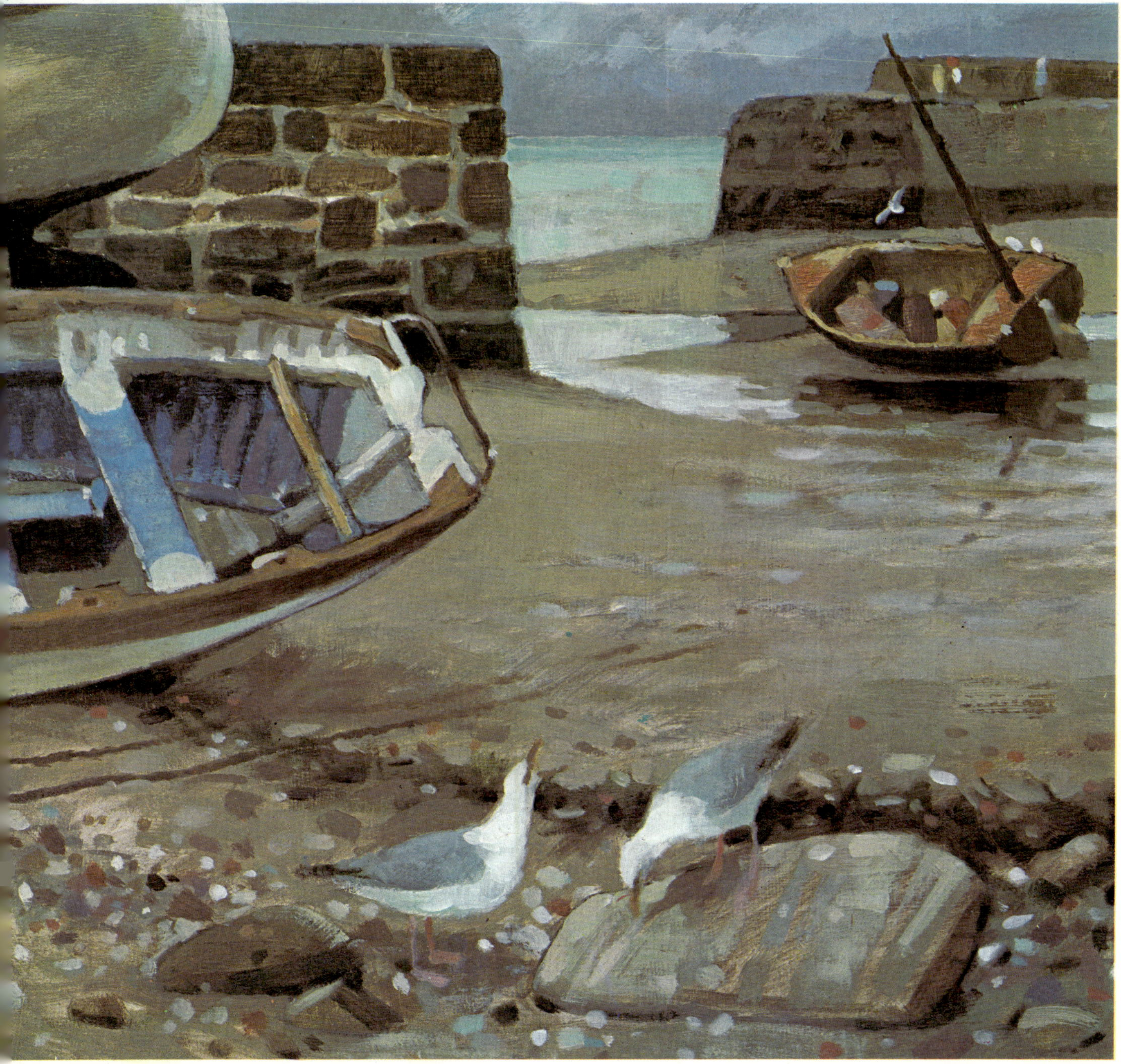

Pleasure and sailing boats

Whether we live inland or on the sea most of us have seen sailing dinghies and other sailcraft about on lakes, rivers and along the coast. Nowadays, their hulls are made of glass fibre which can be moulded in any colour: likewise sailmakers cut sails of material in many colours. The sight of such craft always gives me (and many people) the itch to paint them: they are one of the most popular of subjects with artists.

The beauty of line and form of most sailing craft is compelling, but careful observation of proportion is vital. We tend to draw or paint what we expect to be the proportions but many craft do not conform to the popular conception of a sailing boat. Two triangles for sails are not always sufficient and the proportion of mast height to length of the hull can prove to be surprising.

The sails of most dinghies and cruisers can be extremely colourful, particularly the large balloon spinnaker sails, for they possess the quality of apparently holding the light. They usually reflect a lot of light from the sky and the sea and consequently close scrutiny is needed to check the extent to which coloured sails are affected by the water reflecting on to them.

Other craft such as the small motor cruisers taking visitors out to visit seal rocks or smugglers' coves can provide lively subjects, particularly if they are 'dressed overall' with small flags with the visitors themselves also providing a large share of the colour.

When painting sailing craft, work out the tonal scheme for your picture right from the start. For instance, if you wish to emphasise the sun striking the light sails, your sky and sea or whatever the background consists of must be dark enough to help the sails show up clearly. It can be exaggerated of course but beware of going too far or you may give the painting a rather brash, vulgar look. On the other hand you may wish to keep the whole background light and silhouette the shape of the boats against this. Whichever scheme you wish to use, be positive about your picture and think it out a little beforehand, making small tonal sketches to work out your darks and lights.

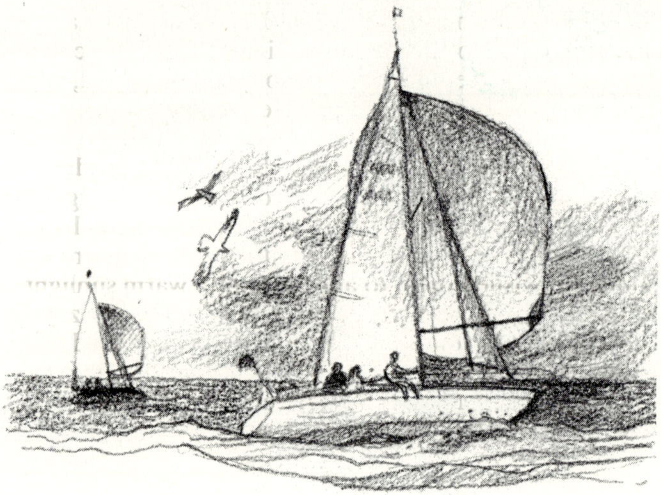

As with all moving objects, sailboats do not compose themselves for your benefit: rarely do you see a satisfying composition for more than a few seconds, which only a camera or the briefest of sketches can record. Try and single out one or two boats at the most for your composition: a row of equally sized shapes can make for a dull picture. An amalgam of your sketches, drawn up carefully, together with colour notes, can provide you with a much more satisfactory picture to paint at home or in the studio.

Dinghy racing: demonstration

Size: 266 × 193 mm/10½ × 7 in. Brushes: Nos. 2 and 6 flat hog-hair; No. 2 flat sable, rigger. Colours: cobalt blue, ultramarine, alizarin crimson, cadmium red, cadmium yellow, yellow ochre, Naples yellow.

For this sailing race (pages 20–1) I wanted to produce a light, sunny atmosphere but, in order to show the light in the sails, I have made sure that the sky has virtually no white and is in fact quite a strong tone. The sails are not white as I wished them to appear lit by a warm sunlight. Although the sky changes colour from top to horizon it does not change tone appreciably. This gives a good tone background not only for the large sails but for the small distant craft on the left whose sails stand out brightly even though they are some way away.

Stage 1 ***(page 20)***

I draw in the subject carefully, paying attention to proportion and avoiding confusing detail where possible, working from a series of preliminary sketches.

Stage 2

I relate the colour and some of the tonal qualities as soon as possible but keep the effect rather lighter than is going to be the case eventually. It is always possible to intensify and strengthen the colour later.

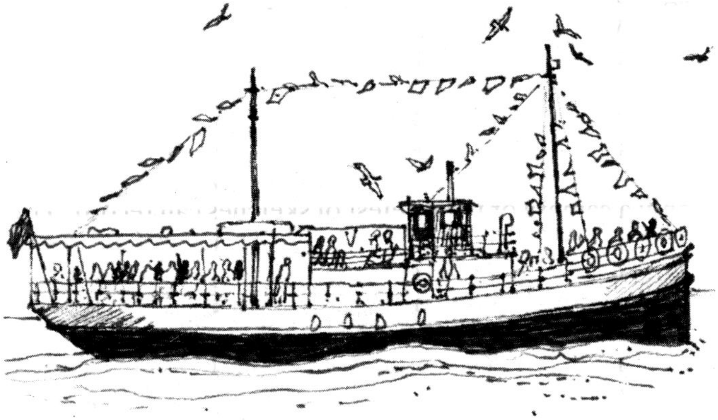

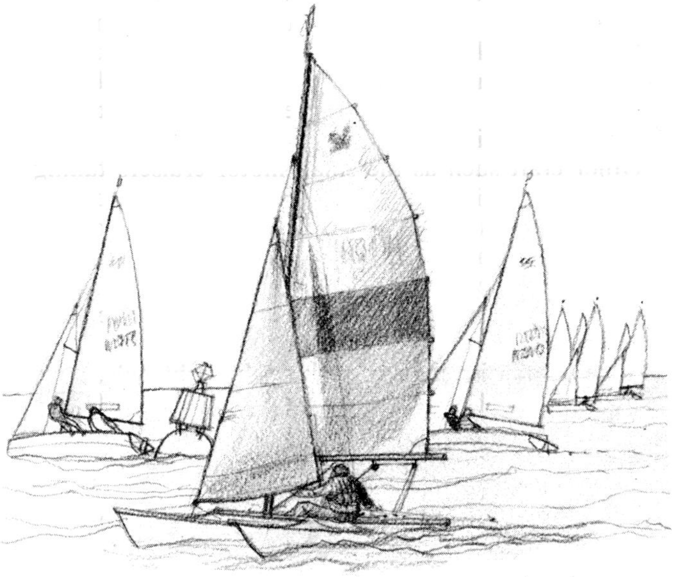

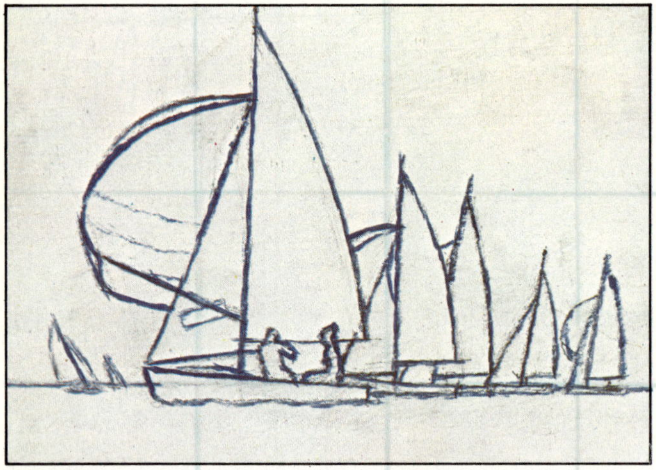

Stage 1

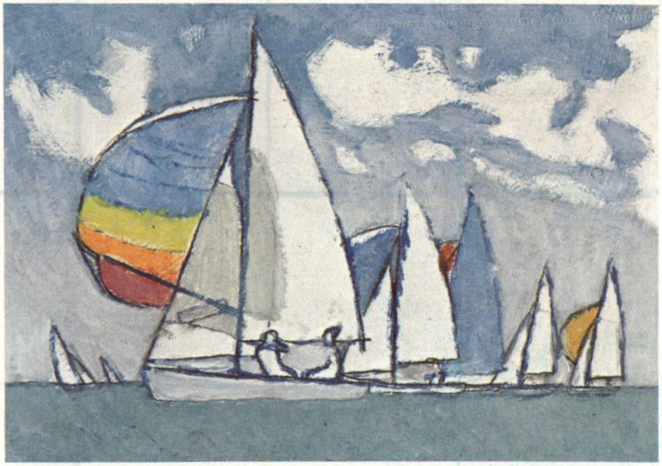

Stage 2

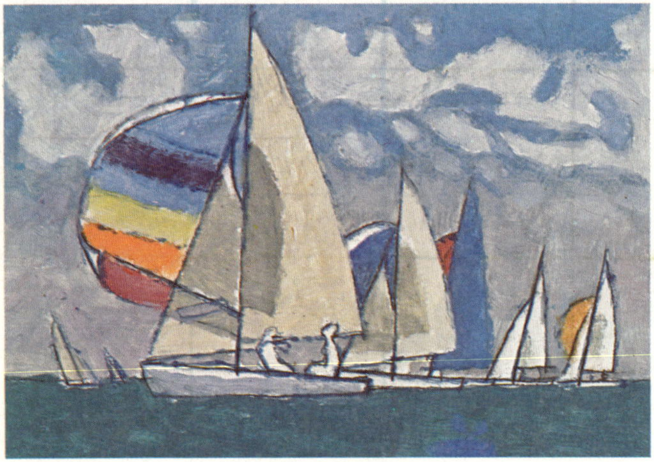

Stage 3

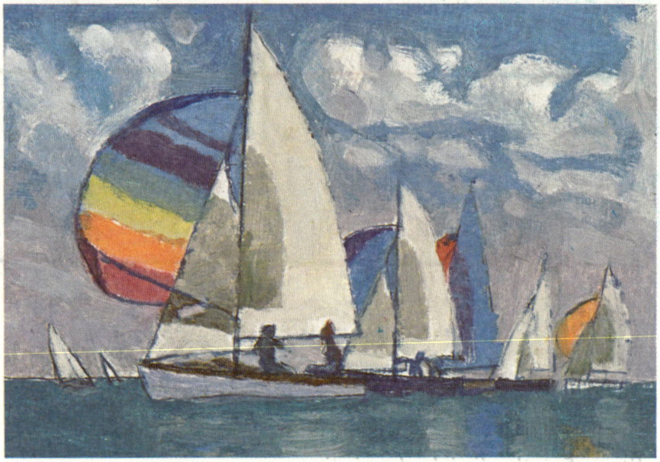

Stage 4

Stage 3

The sky needs to recede, so I brush in the clouds with a soft blue grey, increasing the strength of sky colour near the horizon and the colour on the sails, and darkening the water to achieve the final tonal quality for the whole painting.

Stage 4

I now put in more modelling in the clouds and strengthen the blue of the sky, taking account of the subtlety in the colour of sails, boat hulls and some reflections.

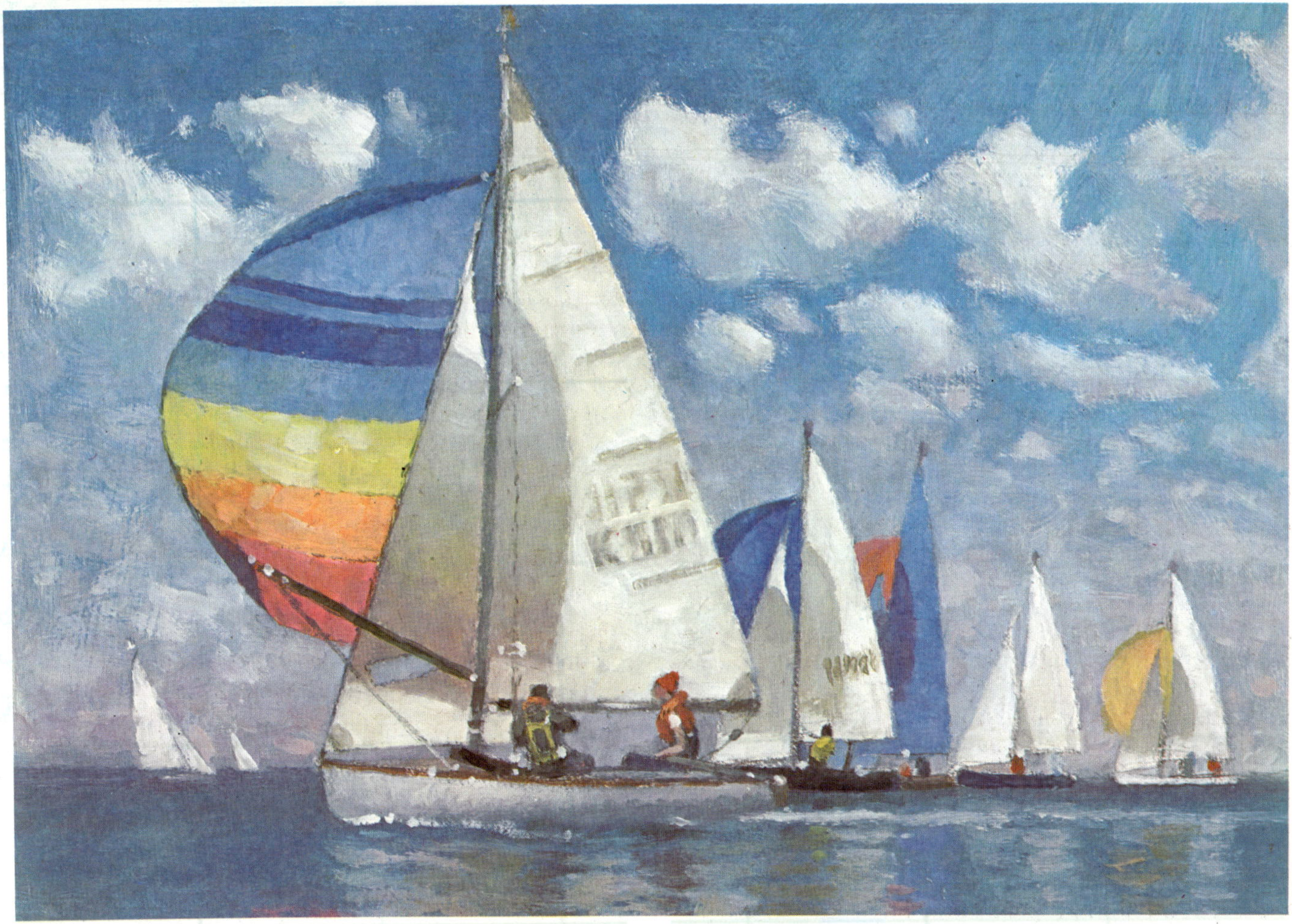

Stage 5 – the finished painting

Stage 5 – the finished painting

This is the point at which the whole painting needs to be balanced up. I lighten the sky and warm it up toward the right as the sun would be just outside the picture on this side. Not only is the sky lightened but a degree of 'warming-up' of the pale blue is necessary through the addition of a little Naples yellow.

I indicate detail, rather than actually paint it in, by the use of various small highlights and carefully placed spots of colour.

Note how I keep the reflections deliberately subdued, so as not to unbalance the picture. Nevertheless, there is a variety of colours in this calm sea to make it interesting.

Docks and Ports

As many of us live in cities I have included a dock scene. A busy port or dock area provides a wealth of material for the keen-eyed painter and, while there is usually a total absence of natural forms, the buildings, cranes, high quaysides; the bustle of containers and goods being loaded or unloaded onto lorries or railway trucks; and the massive curved shapes of cargo ships all offer subjects very different from the little fishing ports illustrated in previous demonstrations, but equally rewarding.

One of the first things one notices about any industrial area, compared with that of clean windswept coastal places, is that the light is almost always different in quality. Smoke and heat haze from towns and cities filters light in a way that can soften the overall colouring. This is not a disadvantage, for industrial machinery, warehouses, ships and dockside fitments are often painted in bright colours, and the atmosphere can have an effect in unifying a scene you might want to paint. I like particularly to contrast the sharp angles of cranes and warehouses with the curved bulk of cargo vessels.

Make sure when you start industrial dockside sketching or painting that you are not in a position that gets in the way of traffic or people's work. Often a good vantage for a picture turns out to be on private property: it is well to obtain permission so that you are not interrupted!

When you have chosen your site, you will probably find that what you can see in front of you has too much material in it: containers may be stacked obscuring part of a ship, a lorry may be too prominent in the foreground. Walk about before settling down, making quick sketches of parts of your subject. Above all, pay attention to the scale of your picture and decide out of the many objects there which ones you wish to be the focus of attention: there is nothing wrong in making the side of a warehouse or the stern of a cargo vessel occupy a large part of your canvas so long as it serves your composition and is interesting in itself. Your preliminary sketches will help you here. Remember that, in subjects such as dock scenes, too much detail can make your final picture look fussy and over-worked: but do try to include people for they give a sense of scale to your subject.

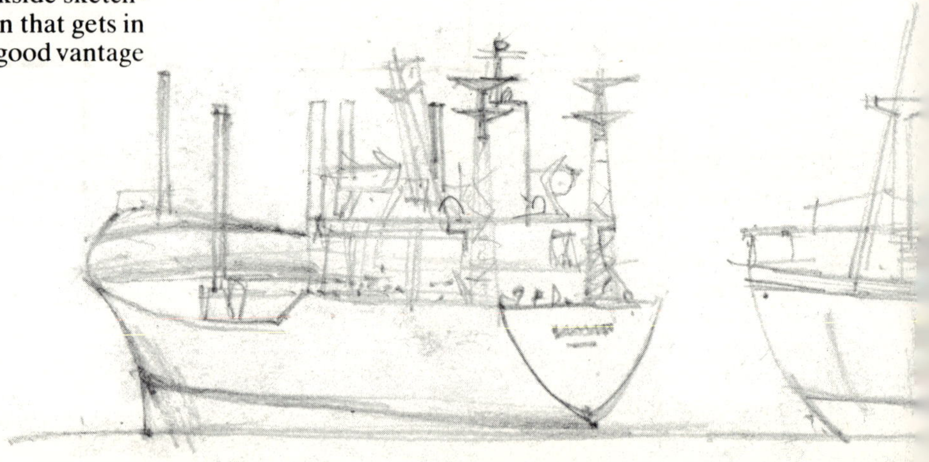

Dock Scene

Size: 265 × 190 mm/10½ × 7½ in. Brushes: Nos. 2 and 6 hog-hair; No. 2 flat sable, rigger. Colours: cobalt blue, ultramarine, sap green, Naples yellow, yellow ochre, raw umber, raw sienna, cadmium orange.

An overcast sky further darkened with industrial smoke sets the tone for this scene (pages 24–5). Nevertheless there is enough shape and colour in the subject for me to want to paint it. Before starting, I walk about the quay-side and make several sketches, before choosing this particular viewpoint. I then find I have to rearrange the large crate in the foreground so that it balances my composition more satisfactorily.

When you tackle an industrial scene such as this, establish the main forms of your composition before you add any detail. Check on your perspective – with all the flat and vertical planes one finds here, an inaccurate line to your vanishing point will soon show up!

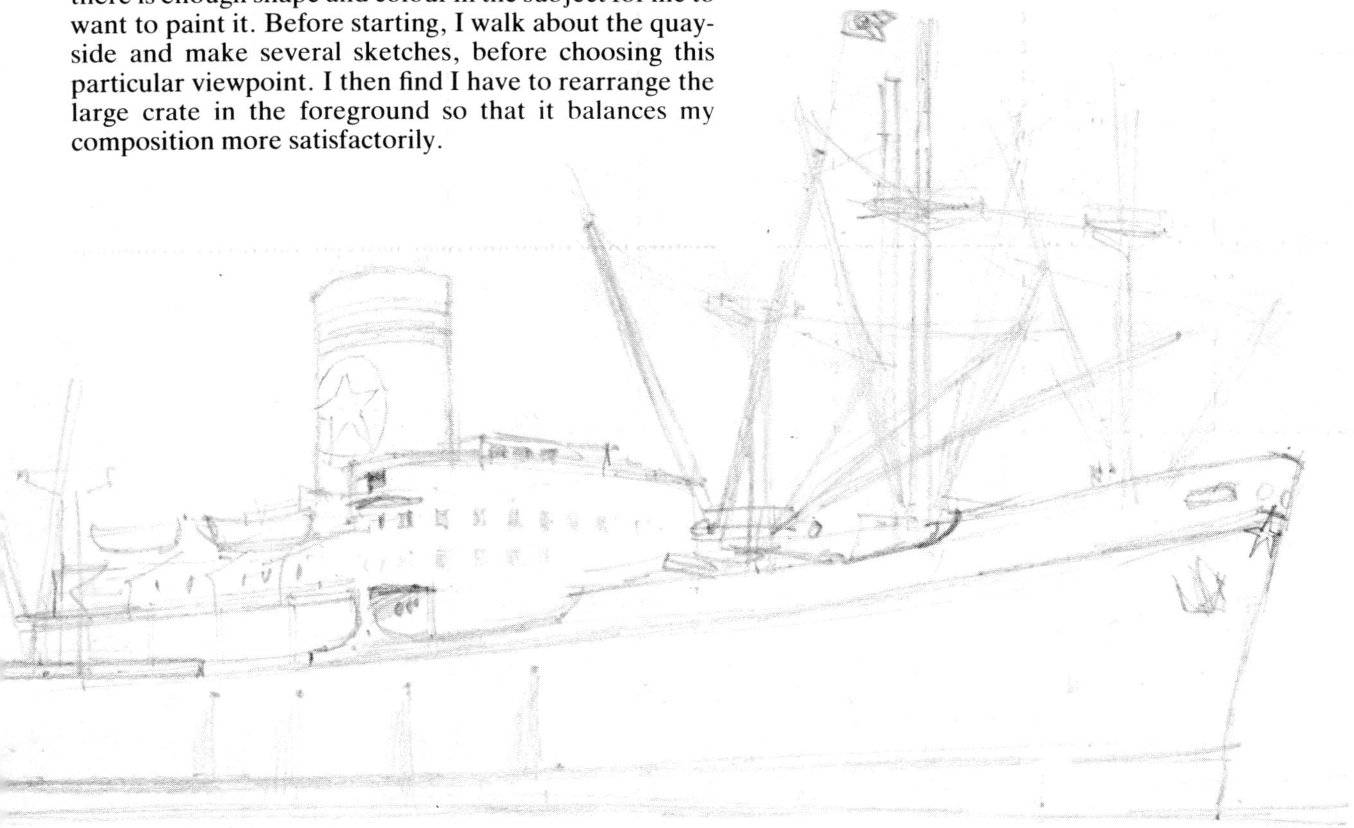

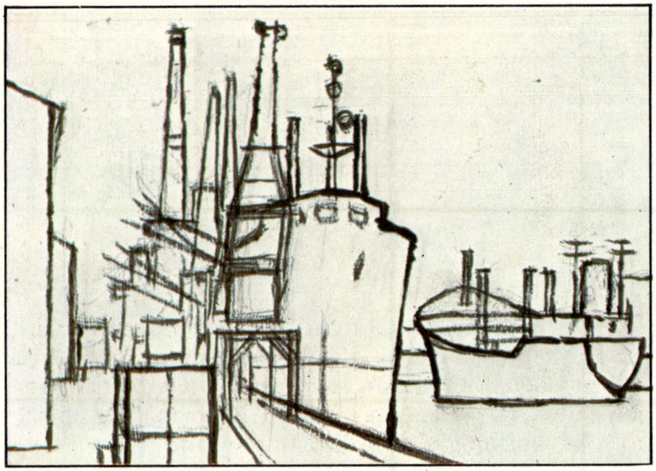

Stage 1

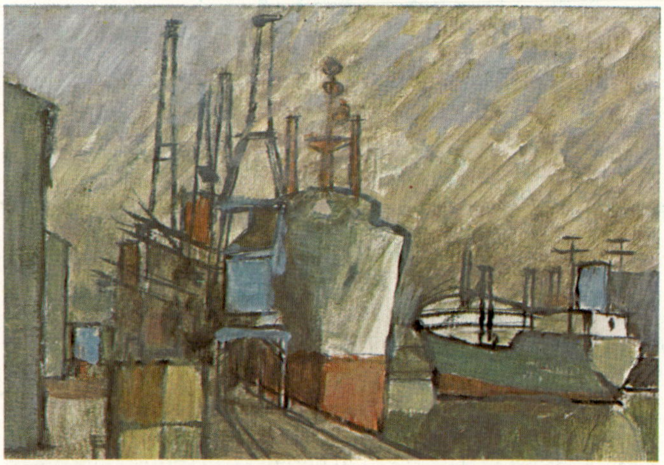

Stage 2

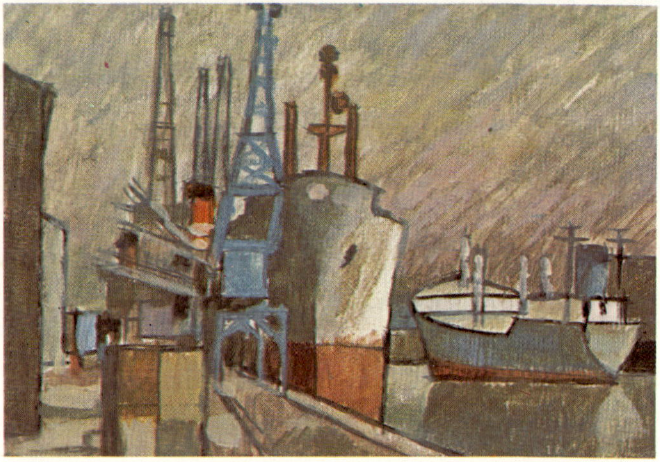

Stage 3

Dock scene: demonstration

Stage 1

After selecting my viewpoint from preliminary sketches I draw in carefully the main outlines, making sure that the perspective lines of the dockside are in accordance with the vanishing point (just above and to the left of the foreground crate). Throughout the painting of this picture I constantly refer to my sketches.

Stage 2

I block in the main tones of the picture, keeping the colours muted at this stage. I establish the colour and tone of the sky, for this gives the key to the overall effect I have in mind for the finished picture.

Stage 3

Still keeping the painting loose within the guidelines established in Stage 1, I gradually work in the detail and smaller forms. (A brilliant yellow forklift truck parked itself at this point in the foreground: I consider for a moment adding it in but decide that it unbalances the colour composition.)

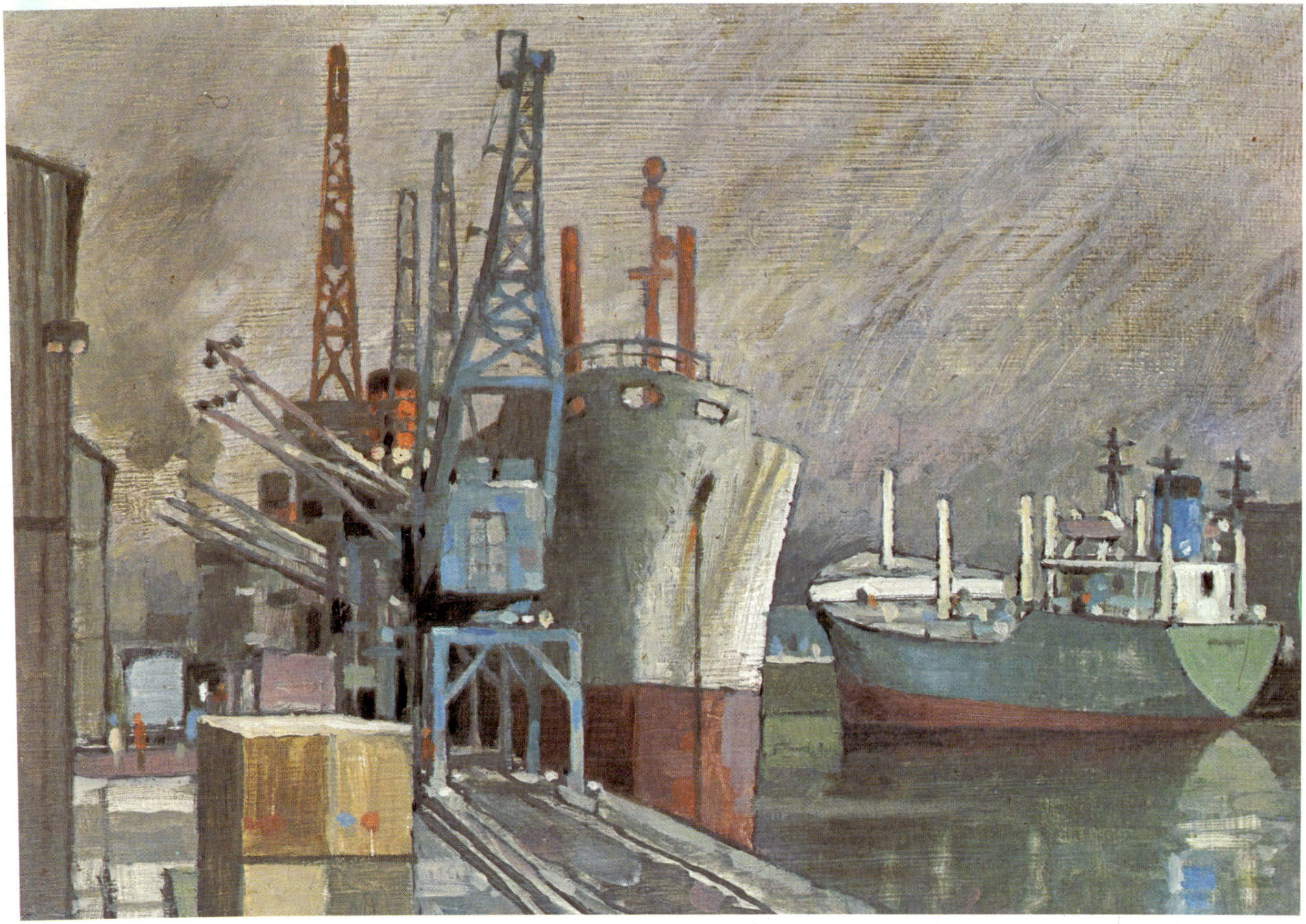

Stage 4 – the finished painting

Stage 4 – the finished painting

At this stage I have to consider just how much detail – of rigging, cranes, lorries and people – I should add without destroying the overall unity of the picture. The reflections of the right-hand vessel are put in (or taken out of wet paint so that the ground showed through). The warmest hue in the picture is the orange funnel and, beneath it, is the centre of the picture's focus. Once I have established this focal point I can choose how much detail to put in below.

A fitful sun was shining dully through the haze, just enough to be caught by the ships' superstructure and hull and also on the sharp edges of the crane in the foreground.

A few figures on the quayside on the left of the picture are suggested with a couple of simple brush strokes in order to provide the overall scale of the subject.

Details of boats and accessories

Nets, floats, lobster pots, boxes, baskets, markers, buoys, chains, anchors, propellers, ropes, blocks and tackle, lights, lifebelts and many more such objects are to be found on or attached to boats or in the vicinity of harbours.

Their variety, surface quality, and basic functional purpose make them fascinating to observe, draw and paint; while they are always useful too as foreground material – a form of still life – in larger pictures.

The effect of sea water, weather and usage tends to add to the visual quality of these objects rather than destroying it. Even when discarded and decaying they exhibit qualities which the boat and harbour painter can put to good use.

Drawing these items can be difficult and exacting, but rewarding if you are going to paint them subsequently. Drawing is the best means of simplifying and finding out how these items function or are put together.

'Stalk' your object – walk around it; handle it and observe it from as many angles as possible before drawing it. Use your drawing ability to clarify and to define its function so that when you come to paint it you understand what you are drawing.

As in many boat details – such as rigging, nets, rope, and other linear objects – it is necessary to paint these using a rigger or fine, round sectioned sable brush. However, the result can often look hard or fussy and out of scale with the rest of the painting. There are two good ways to combat this. One is to avoid using too dark a tone on these details. The other is to paint the lines rather thicker than finally required and then paint back the background between the lines using a similar brush to the rest of the painting, slightly cutting back or overlapping the lines. This method relates the line work to the general scale of the other brush work and gives a looser effect.

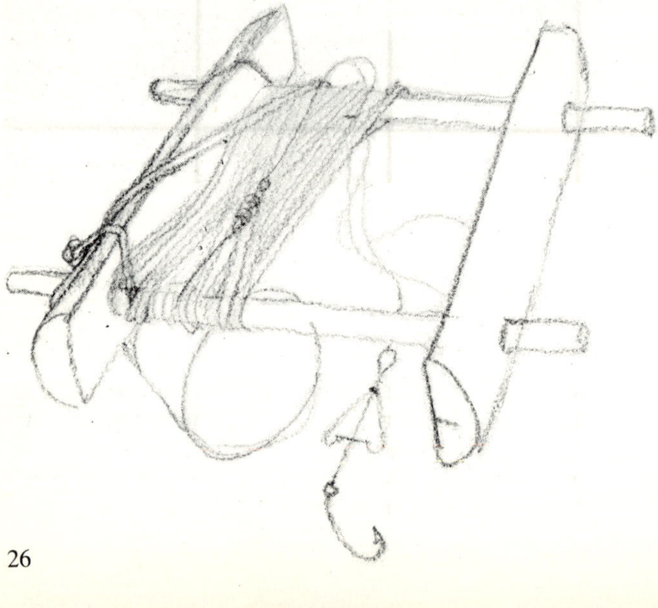

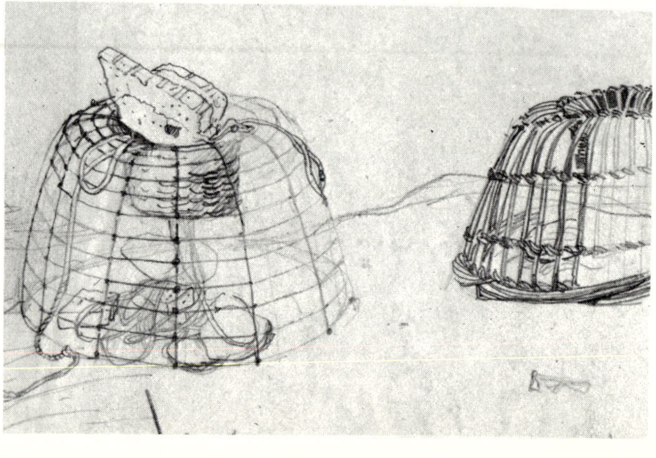

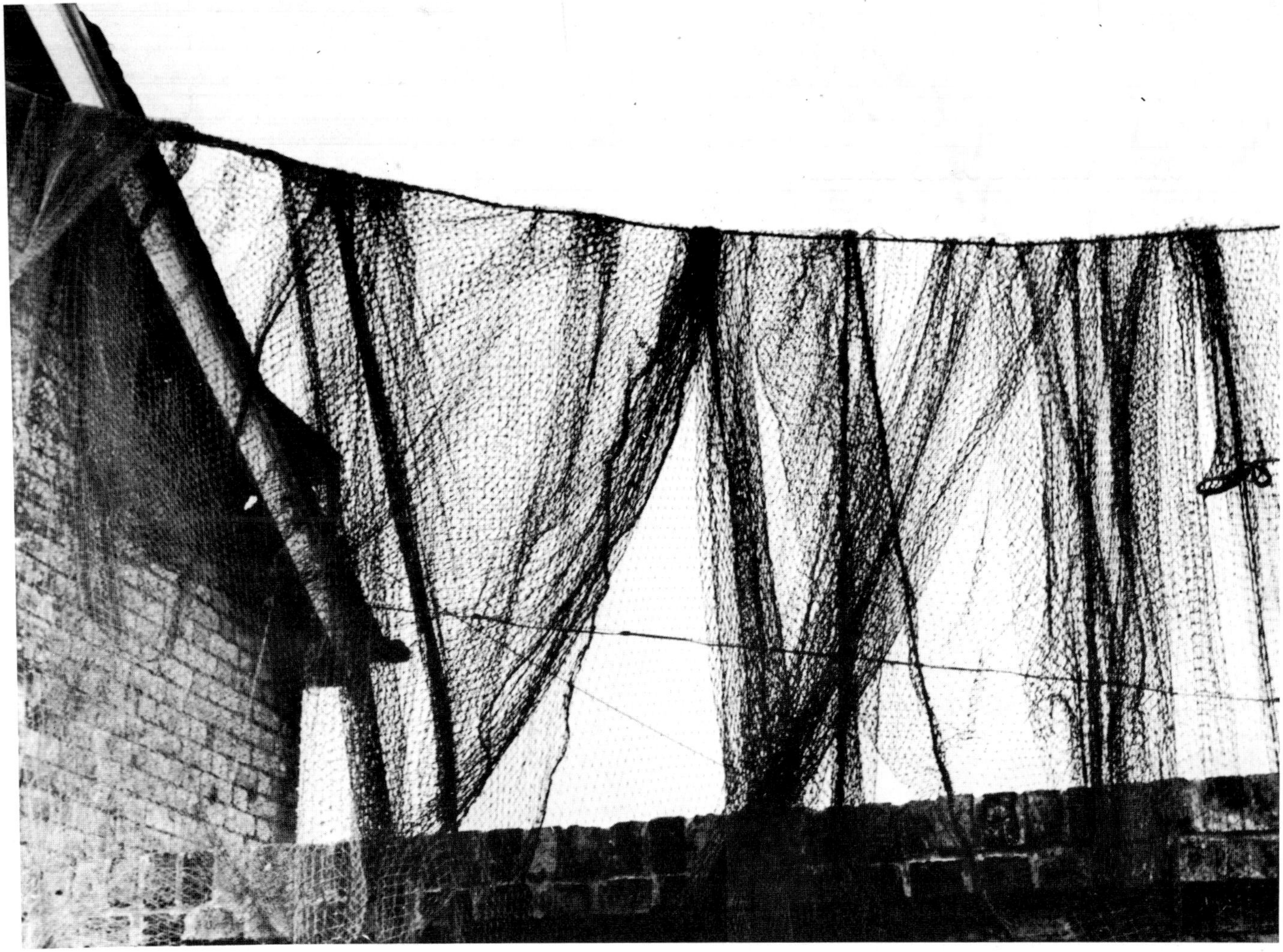

Using photographs

As I have already pointed out, a camera is helpful in recording the moving aspects of marine subjects – sailboats and fishing vessels. But accessories too get moved about from one day to the next: a pile of lobster pots on a quay you see one evening will be gone the next day, nets likewise. This photograph has a linear quality that captures my imagination; I like the way the nets are draped. It was from such a photograph that once, on a very rainy day, I painted a 'composed' picture of freshly-caught mackerel. See page 32.

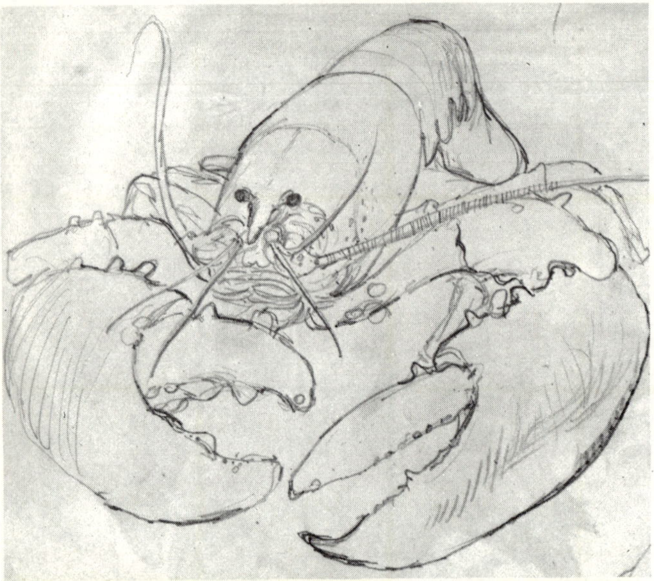

On the Beach: demonstration

Size: 265 × 190 mm/10½ × 7½ in. Brushes: Nos. 2 and 6 flat hog-hair; No. 4 sable, rigger. Colours: raw sienna, raw umber, Indian red, cobalt blue, cadmium red, yellow ochre, Naples yellow.

When painting a subject composed of details such as these, do consider the colour and tone of the individual elements in relation to the background. Are they lighter, warmer, cooler, darker? Do their shapes contrast interestingly with each other and with the background of larger forms? Avoid including too many objects which might cancel out each others' qualities. Better to concentrate on two or three details which have visual characteristics different from each other. The firm clean roundness of propeller blades against the angularity and roughness of the rudder and the more delicate net-like quality of the lobster pots gave me such a subject: simple in composition yet interesting in scale and detail. I have also contrasted scale, e.g. the houses behind the beach are smaller in the picture than the propeller and lobster pots, and are dwarfed by the mass of the boat's stern.

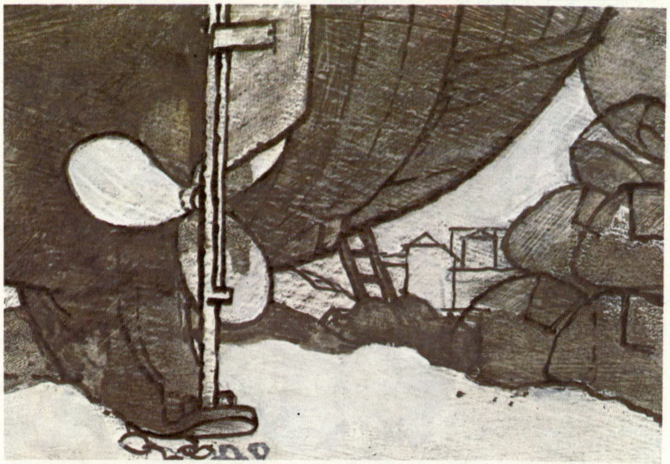

Stage 1

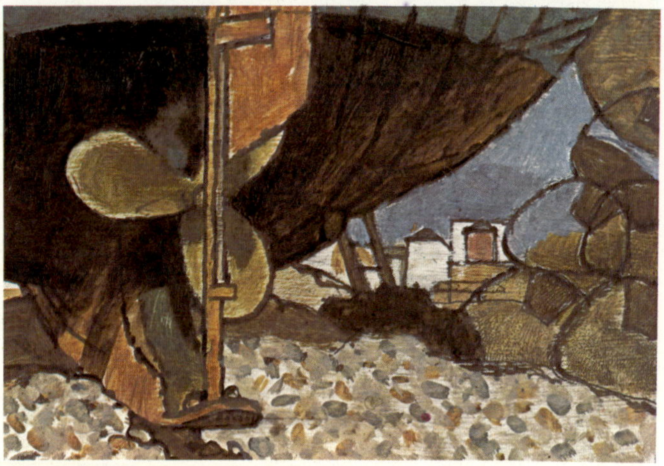

Stage 2

Stage 1

As this composition is so dependent on tonal relationships – the dark mass of the boat, the lightness of the beach texture and the light on the buildings – I indicate a rough approximation in tone at the same time as the drawing-in.

Stage 2

Keeping the shadow areas rich and colourful is important, and for this I have to work out the quality of the

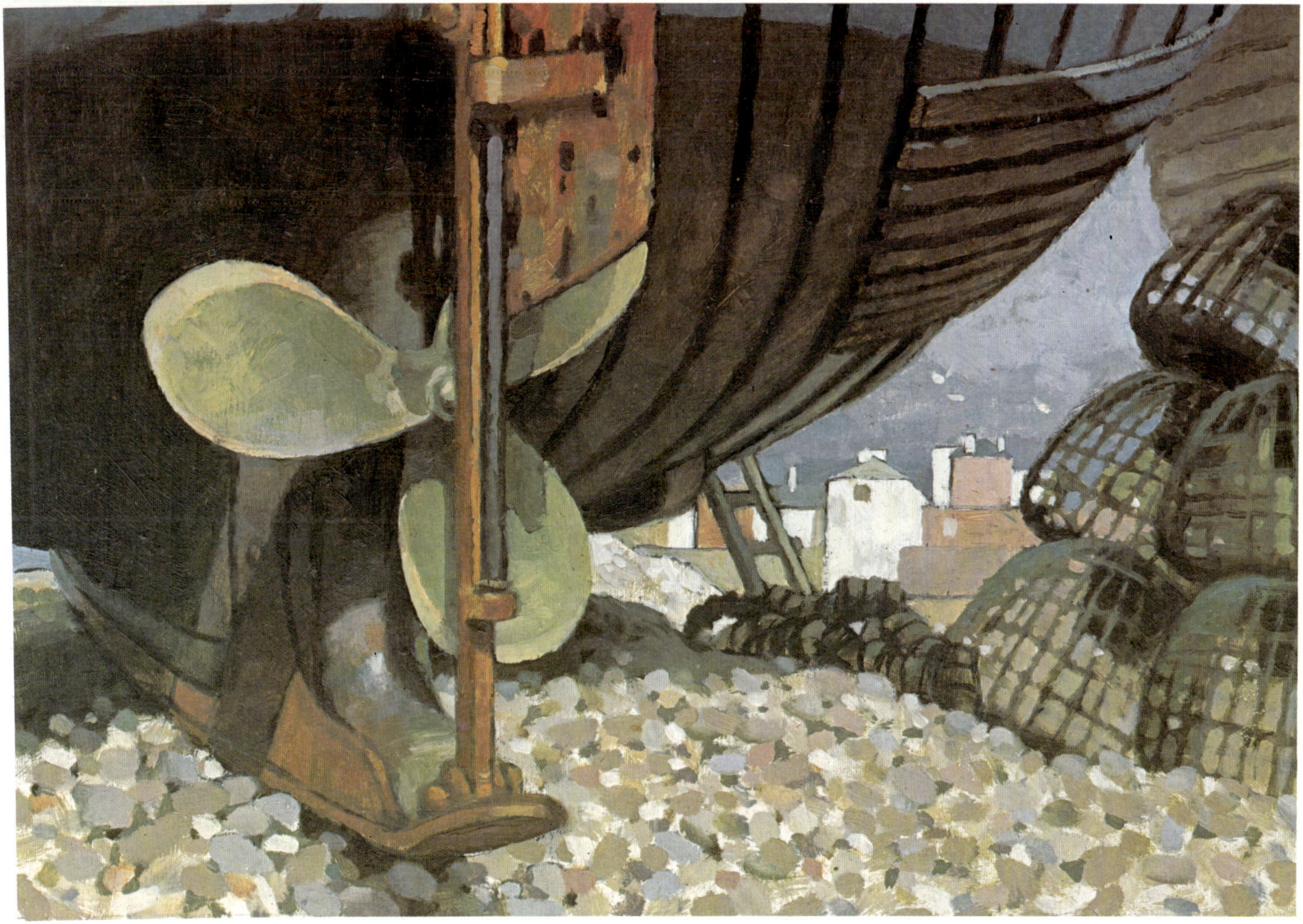

Stage 3 – the finished painting

light. As the boat itself varies from black underside to blue painted boards on the sides it was a little complicated. However, notice that there is a lot of warm reflected light coming up from the light pebbles on the beach. This gives the underside a dark brown glow even on the black of the underwater area of the hull and also warms up the blue of the other boarding.

Stage 3 – the finished painting

I have gone for the surface qualities of the various objects: the smooth sculptural form of the propeller, the rich dark tones of the stern of the boat and the light striking the distant houses, and the texture of the pebbles on the beach. To keep the beach light I only indicate deep shadow between occasional pebbles. This was a sufficient clue to keep the beach texture strong but essentially light in tone.

Structural Boat Drawing

Apart from racing sailboats, it is unusual to find two boats of similar shape and size. Boats are built to suit the work they do, and when looked at are never arranged like matches in a match box. Even when you are drawing or painting boats in the water, a knowledge of their total structure, including that part hidden by the water, is an advantage. It is appropriate to end this book by giving a few pointers on looking at boat forms from different angles, and on how best to go about drawing them.

Boat hulks, as I have said, are very sculptural, and if you imagine them, not as constructed out of bent planks but as the whole boat carved from a solid block of material, then you will understand my approach.

Visualise the boat you wish to draw or paint as first having been in the form of a brick, or large baulk of timber. By 'seeing' this rectangular shape first, you will naturally draw it in perspective as you would a house or building. Very lightly draw in the appropriate 'box' for your first boat, making sure your perspective lines are consistent with your overall picture. If your boat is tilted, or lying on its side, then your 'box' should take up the same angle. Similarly, if you are viewing your boat from the stern, or three-quarters on, so your 'box' must take on the same viewpoint. Now, by drawing your boat within the 'box', you can 'carve' it down by seeing the lines, bulk and shape. Where inward curves show up, so the 'box' is cut away: in other places, the sides of the boat and the keel will touch the outer sides, top, bottom and ends of your 'box'. On this page and opposite are simple outline drawings of a typical small fishing boat drawn from four different viewpoints: plan, elevation, stern on, and three-quarters stern on. Notice how perspective plays an essential part of the construction in the two on the right.

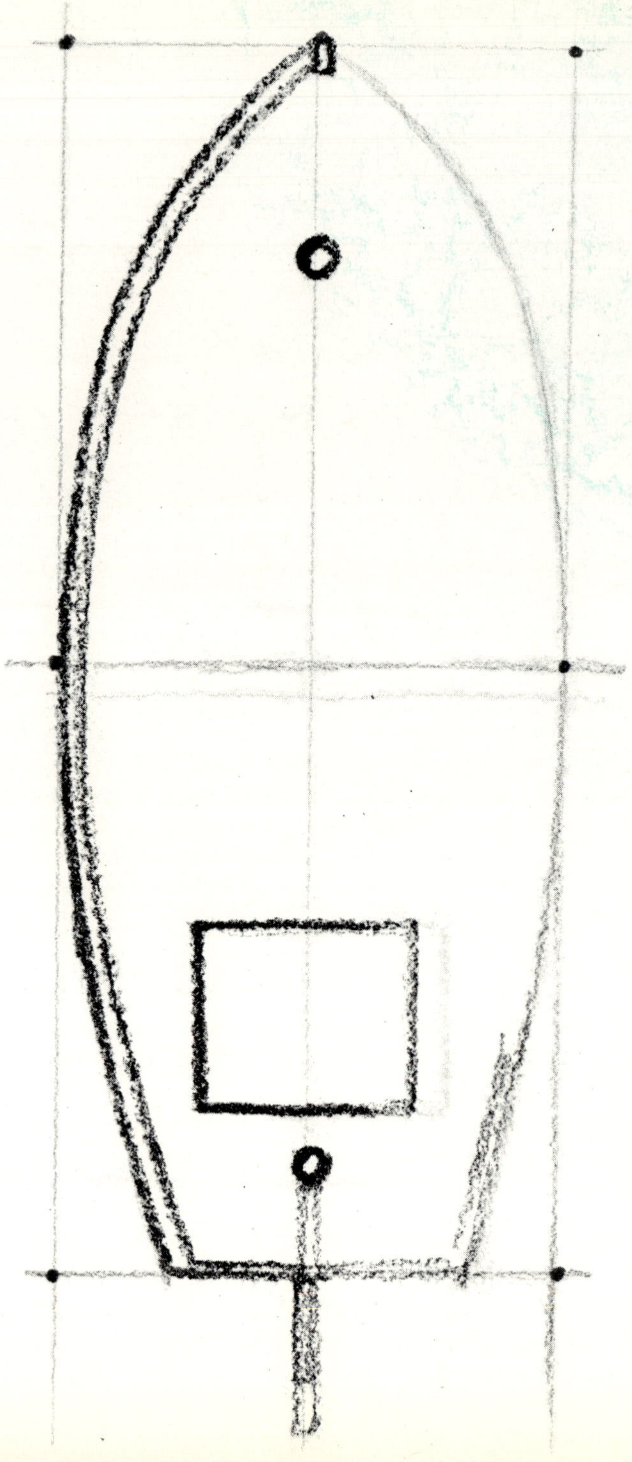

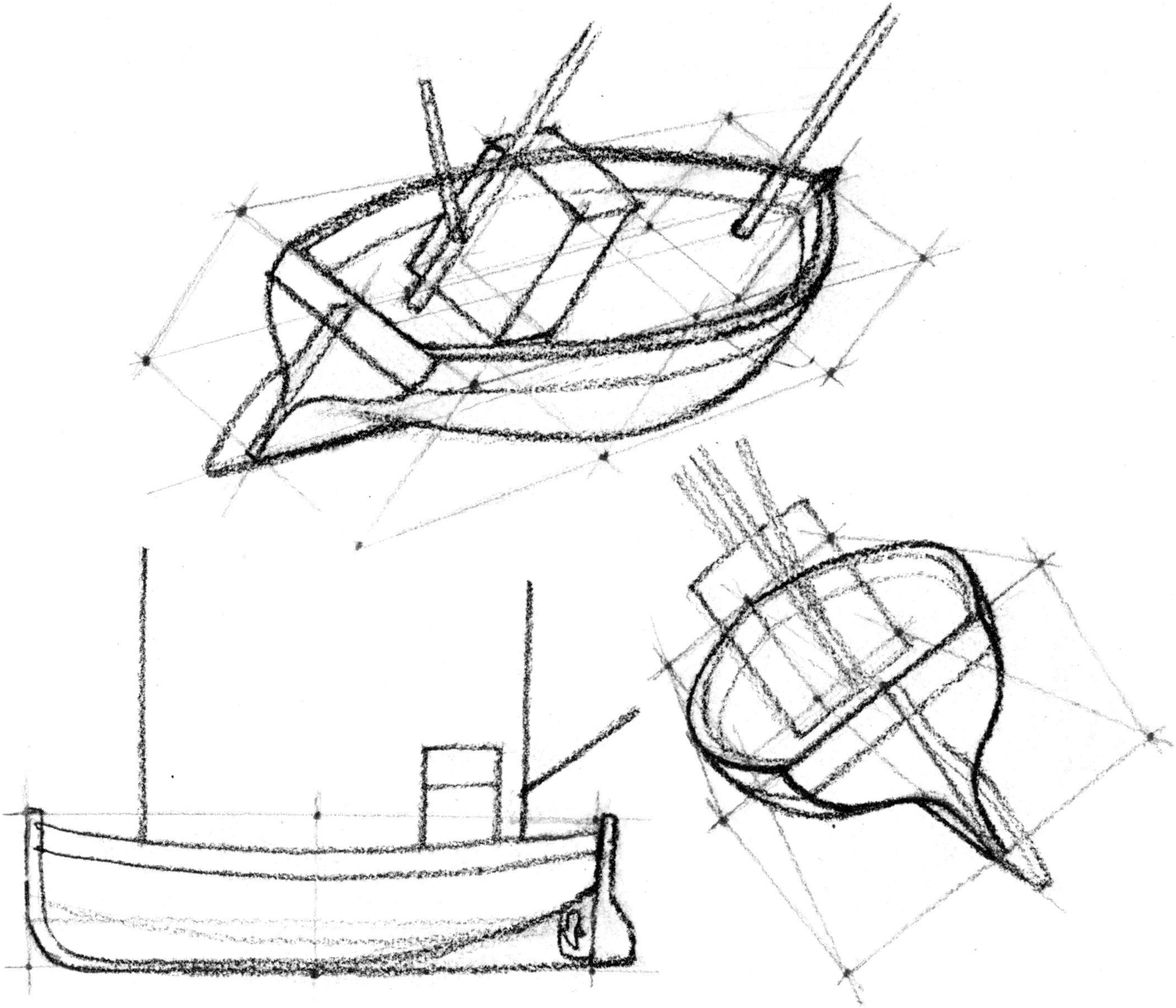

Visualise the boat you wish to draw as first having been in the form of a brick, or a large baulk of timber. See opposite, and page 2.

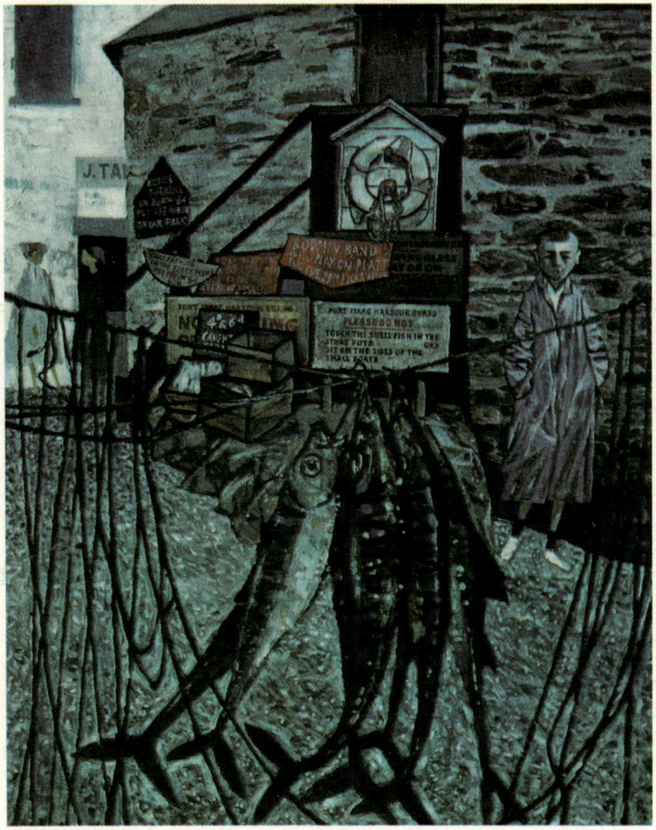

A rainy day, Port Isaac

This picture was painted from memory, but I also used photographs to build up the pictorial elements. I possessed photographs of the buildings and the street, I had made a quick sketch (in the rain) of the main figure. I also had from another occasion a watercolour sketch of the mackerel strung on a line. From these several sources I drew a composition sketch from which this picture was painted.

ACKNOWLEDGEMENTS

Text, drawings and paintings by Clifford Bayly.

First published in Great Britain in 1982 by Search Press Limited, Wellwood, North Farm Road, Tunbridge Wells, Kent TN2 3DR

First published in the United States in 1982 by Taplinger Publishing Co., Inc., New York, New York.

First published in Australia in 1982 by Methuen Australia Pty Ltd, 44 Waterloo Road, North Ryde, NSW 2113

National Library of Australia
Cataloguing-in-Publication data

Bayly, Clifford.
Painting boats and harbours in oils
Simultaneously published: London: Search Press.
1. Marine painting – Technique. 2. Ships in art.
3. Harbors in art. I. Title. (Series: Leisure arts; 14).

751.45′437

UK ISBN 0 85532 457 0
US ISBN 0 8008 6208 2
Aust ISBN 0 454 00476 1

Made and printed in Italy by L.E.G.O. Vicenza